MAUD'S HOUSE OF DREAMS

ALSO BY JANET LUNN

The Root Cellar
Shadow in Hawthorn Bay
The Hollow Tree
The Story of Canada (with Christopher Moore)

MAUD'S HOUSE OF DREAMS

The Life of Lucy Maud Montgomery

Janet Lunn

Doubleday Canada

National Library of Canada Cataloguing in Publication Data

Lunn, Janet, 1928–
Maud's house of dreams : the life of Lucy Maud Montgomery / Janet Lunn.

ISBN 0–385–65933–4

1. Montgomery, L. M. (Lucy Maud), 1874–1942—Biography—Juvenile literature. 2. Novelists, Canadian (English)—20th century—Biography—Juvenile literature. I. Title.

PS8526.O55Z7935 2002   jC813.'52   C2002-901309-7
PR9199.3.M6Z7935 2002

Jacket photograph: courtesy George Campbell, L. M. Montgomery Museum, Silver Bush
Jacket photo hand-tinting: Troy Hill-Jackson
Jacket design: Counterpunch/Linda Gustafson
Text design: Leah Springate
Printed and bound in the USA

Published in Canada by
Doubleday Canada, a division of
Random House of Canada Limited

Visit Random House of Canada Limited's website: www.randomhouse.ca

BVG   10 9 8 7 6 5 4 3 2 1

This book is in memory of Lucy Maud Montgomery, and for Elizabeth Moore, who has loved her books more than anyone I have ever known.

TABLE OF CONTENTS

CHAPTER I

Story Girl

" . . . she could see it plainly with its turrets and banners on the pine-clad mountain height, wrapped in its fain, blue loveliness, against the sunset skies of a fair and unknown land. Everything wonderful and beautiful was in that castle."—THE BLUE CASTLE

Maud Montgomery was not quite two years old when she saw her mother for the last time. Dressed in a lace-trimmed white muslin dress, held tightly in her father's arms, she looked down at the beautiful face in the coffin. She could feel her father's tears on her cheeks. She could hear someone in the room sobbing. Outside the open parlour window behind the sofa across the room, a breeze was making the bright green vines dance. She leaned down and put her hand on Mama's face. It was cold. She turned and buried her face in her father's neck. As young as she was, she remembered every detail of that moment all her life.

That sad scene was revisited over and over again in the books the grown-up Maud wrote: Emily Starr crying her heart out on her father's coffin in *Emily of New Moon*, Marigold Lesley imagining her father's dead face in *Magic for Marigold*.

But those books came many years later and the journey from the day her mother was buried to the day Maud wrote "Lucy Maud Montgomery" at the end of her first published story was long and often painful.

Maud was born on November 30, 1874 in the tiny hamlet of Clifton (now New London) on an inlet along the north shore of Prince Edward Island. The cradle-shaped island, the smallest province in Canada, is a soft and beautiful place where the sea wind blows almost constantly over the rolling green hills and the white farm houses. The island is just over two hundred kilometres long and sixty kilometres wide at its widest spot (only four at its narrowest). It lies in the Gulf of the St. Lawrence, just off the coasts of Nova Scotia and New Brunswick. Hundreds of years ago, when the Miqmaq people were the only people who lived there, they named it *Abegweit,* which means cradled on the waves. More often, they called it *Minagoo* which means, simply, the island. Centuries later, when the the French owned the island, they named it *Ile St Jean* but they, too, more often just called it *l'ile,* the island. By the time Maud Montgomery was born, the island was part of Canada and was officially named Prince Edward Island, but it was still just the Island to its people, as though there were no other in the world.

The hills rise highest along the Island's north shore near Cavendish. They end in steep, rust-red sandstone cliffs that drop down onto rocks and towering sand dunes at the edge of the sea. Back from the cliffs, the roads, as red as the rocks and the cliff sides, wind among farms and meadows, through woods and along bubbling brooks. When Maud was growing up there were no telephone poles or wires strung along those red dirt roads, no cars on them, and no airplanes droned overhead. Instead there were wagons and carts, buggies and fashionable carriages, pulled by horses clip-clopping on the roads and only birds flew overhead. There were great sailing ships and steamships in the big harbours of Sunnyside and Charlottetown and fishing boats in every small harbour and cove and along all the beaches. Trains chugged along the narrow-gauge tracks that zig-zagged through the province, their shrill whistles loudly announcing their arrivals and departures at the stations along the way. In 1873, only a year before Maud was born, the Island had become the newest province in Canada and Maud's grandfather, Donald Montgomery, had been named its first member of the Canadian senate.

None of this meant anything to the baby who was baptised Lucy Maud Montgomery in the Presbyterian church in Cavendish, where her mother's people lived. She was named Lucy for her mother's mother and Maud for one of the daughters of Queen Victoria but she was never called either Lucy or Lucy Maud. She was always just Maud—or Maudie to her father.

Hugh John Montgomery and his wife Clara Macneill Montgomery had been happy with their new baby in their little yellow house in Clifton. Hugh John was a storekeeper there and Clara kept house, dropping her work every few minutes to croon over her golden-haired, bright-eyed baby. Maud later put her own daydreams about the Clifton house into *Anne of Green Gables* when Anne imagined her mother's and father's little yellow house with "honeysuckle over the parlour window and lilacs in the front yard . . ." But bliss soon turned to sorrow when Clara fell ill with tuberculosis and had to go home to Cavendish to be cared for by her mother. A few months later she died there.

A heart-broken Hugh John left Maud with her Macneill grandparents. The store in Clifton was bankrupt and he needed to be free to move wherever work took him. When he settled again, he told Maud's grandparents, he would have his Maudie to live with him. But he did not soon settle and the bed Grandmother Macneill had made up for Maud in the little room off the sitting room in the big farmhouse became hers for all her growing years.

So, in a way, Maud Montgomery was as much an orphan as Anne Shirley, or Emily Starr, the heroines of her imagination, with an absent father she adored as Jane Stuart did hers in *Jane of Lantern Hill*. She was a small, spindly, sparrow of a child with long, straight, gold-brown hair usually pulled back from her small, intense face in two tight braids. She had a delicate mouth and nose and clear grey eyes that noticed everything around her. She had the same sharp, determined chin she gave both Anne and Emily and she, too, could have been described as "elfin." She was quick-witted and clever and she felt every pleasure and every pain so keenly that life was a constant succession of acute joys and griefs.

Maud was like both Anne and Emily, too, in that she loved big, interesting words and was always making up stories—even before she could read and write. She had the kind of imagination that could change her everyday world into a beautiful and magical realm or, as readily, into one that was ugly and terrifying. She believed—as Anne did—that the gossamer webs on the delicate fern leaves on dewy mornings were fairy tablecloths and, then, when her grandmother locked her in the dark spare room for punishment, as Aunt Elizabeth did Emily, the room was instantly full of "great black hands" and grey, menacing shapes.

Often she would curl up by the upstairs window, or out in a corner of the barn with a cat in her lap, far from anyone's notice. She would dream, like Valancy Stirling, that the old Cavendish farmhouse—with its dark parlour, its plain kitchen, and its sitting room where Grandfather sat frowning over his newspaper—had become a blue castle full of light and love and she its princess, the daughter of young, beautiful parents who cherished her.

She was more tolerated than cherished by her aunt and her grandparents. Aunt Emily was young and pretty and lively. Possibly she was a lot like Aunt Olivia in *The Story Girl*, "just like a pansy, all velvety, and purply and goldy." She would sometimes play games with Maud or read to her, but usually, when she wasn't busy with household chores, she was out at Sewing Circle or Bible Study or visiting with friends. And, all too often, she scolded Maud for being too noisy, too untidy, *too* almost everything.

Grandmother and Grandfather Macneill were already past middle age. All of their six children but Emily had married and left home. They had no wish to raise another one, but a strong sense of duty made them take in their dead daughter's child. Furthermore, Grandfather's stern Scottish pride insisted that Macneills "looked after their own."

Grandfather, Alexander Macneill, had deep-set eyes under bushy eyebrows, white hair, and a white beard that framed his angry-looking face. He was an impatient, bad-tempered man, quick to feel insulted and quick to insult other people. He liked to jab at people with an unkind wit. Giving "digs" or "bars," he called it. Maud held him in great awe and she did her best to keep out of his way except when he was telling stories. Grandfather could tell stories about Macneills long dead and buried that could make you swear they were living breathing people right there in the room with you.

Grandmother, Lucy Woolner Macneill, wasn't a story teller. She was a practical, hard-working woman. She wasn't as frightening as Grandfather, but she wasn't warm and loving, either. In *Emily of New Moon,* when Emily described Aunt Elizabeth, she might have been describing Maud's Grandmother Macneill: "Quite fine looking in a tall, thin, austere style, with clear-cut features and a massive coronet of iron-grey hair under her black lace cap. But her eyes, though steel blue, were cold . . . and her long thin mouth was compressed severely." This was Maud's Grandmother Macneill, right down to the steel, blue eyes.

Cavendish was a small farming community at the edge of the sea. It was about two-and-a-half kilometres long and one-and-a-half wide, with a main road running through it. The Presbyterian and Baptist churches and the school were on that road. The farms were all set back from it. The Alexander Macneill farm was just a short lane up from the main road. It sat on a low hill, with the cook house, the barn, the granary, the chicken house, and the outhouse behind, and apple orchards, potato and corn fields, and the pastures for sheep and cows sloping away in all directions. The big, white clapboard house was built by Maud's great-grandfather.

Inside, the parlour had lace curtains and an elegant carpet patterned with red roses and light-green ferns. It was furnished with stiff, cane-bottomed chairs, a horse hair sofa and upright rocking chairs with bright cushions on their seats and lace "tidies" on their high backs to keep them clean. This room, where her mother had lain in her coffin, never felt like a happy room to Maud. The sitting room, with its big, oval table and its more comfortable chairs, seemed much friendlier. So did the kitchen, always filled with the smell of bread rising, soup cooking, or pies baking, and the comfortable wood fire glowing in the polished black stove. Maud liked the cosy bedroom off the sitting room where she slept in winter when the unheated upstairs was too cold—but her upstairs bedroom was her *real* bedroom. It looked south through the dappled shade of the apple trees toward the "hill field" and it was her private place, her sanctuary, her "own dear den." Also upstairs were Grandmother and Grandfather's bedroom, the spare room, and "the lookout," a tiny room where Maud was allowed to keep her dolls and books and small treasures. This room had a window that looked west toward hills and woods.

Grandfather was not only a farmer, he was the community postmaster. So the farmhouse front room was the post office, where all in Cavendish came, not only to post and pick up their mail, but to catch up on the news. It was an exciting place to be. Maud was so little and thin she could disappear unnoticed into a corner to listen to the gossip. She liked even better to be in the kitchen on the evenings when it was full of visitors. The kettle would be moved to the front of the stove to boil and the teapot would be filled. Then the stories would begin. Everyone had a story, but Grandfather always had the best ones—and told them best. The flowing words in his deep, sonorous voice resounded in Maud's ears for hours afterwards and the stories stayed with her forever.

She would sit there, her knees drawn up to her chin, her arms tight around them, soaking up the stories, her eyes darting eagerly from one speaker to another, until Aunt Emily would espy her and take her off to bed. Then she would lie in bed in her room off the sitting room, where she could still smell the wood burning in the stove, still hear the rhythm of the voices through the closed doors, and she would make up stories to go with the voices.

Sometimes the gatherings in the sitting room or kitchen held no pleasure for her. More than half of the two-hundred-and-some people in Cavendish were Maud's relatives: Macneill, Simpson or Clark aunts, uncles, first, second and third cousins. Maud had thirty-five first cousins, not all living in Cavendish, and more second and third cousins than even Grandfather Macneill could count—all too many of them living in Cavendish. A century earlier, their families had been the first English and Scottish immigrants to the Island. Among them had been poets and story tellers and elders of the Presbyterian Church, educated people who loved literature. Maud's great-grandfather Macneill had been the speaker of the Prince Edward Island House of Assembly back in the 1830s. From her earliest days, Maud was made aware of her family's social position and her duty to that position (her great-aunt Mary Lawson once told her, "the Macneills and the Simpsons always considered themselves a little better than the common run.")

The family's social position wasn't all Maud was made aware of. Almost before she could talk, she was given to understand that she was not quite as good as the other children in the clan. She was a charity child. Her mother was dead. The father she loved so much came often to see her, but he did not contribute much to her upkeep. Her mother's relatives never let her forget that. With no brothers or sisters to defend her, her cousins could torment her freely. With no parents to protect her, there was no one to shield her from Aunt Ann Maria's scorn or Uncle John's bullying. When Aunt Hattie came with Uncle Chester from Charlottetown, which luckily wasn't often, she treated Maud like a stray cat her grandparents had been forced to shelter. Uncle Chester made tiresome jokes, like the ones Valancy Stirling's Uncle Benjamin made in *The Blue Castle,* and otherwise ignored Maud. Uncle Leander, who came to the farm every summer for six weeks with his family, either bullied or ignored her.

Not all the Macneill relatives were hurtful. There were kindhearted grown-up cousins like David and Margaret Macneill and Pierce and Rachel Macneill. There was Great-uncle Jimmy who lived across the road (and may have inspired Emily Starr's Cousin Jimmy). Aunt Annie Campbell and Great-aunt Mary Lawson were truly kind, and Maud loved these aunts with all her passionate heart. But Aunt Annie Campbell lived over twenty kilometres away in Park Corner and Great-aunt Mary Lawson was old and widowed and lived in different homes on the Island, for awhile with one relative, then for awhile with another. Cavendish—and Maud—did not see her often.

Then there were the children. She especially liked Pensie Macneill, who was four years older, and Amanda, who was a year younger, and she liked Lucy, Uncle John and Aunt Ann Maria's daughter. But Maud did not see these children much— or any of her cousins or the neighbourhood children—before her school years, except in church or Sunday school.

None of Maud's Montgomery relatives lived in Cavendish. Grandfather and Grandmother Montgomery lived in Park

Corner and so did most of Maud's relatives on her father's side of her family. Aunt Annie and Uncle John Campbell and their children, Aunt Jane and Uncle Charles Crosby and their children, and other Montgomerys, too numerous to mention, all lived in Park Corner or along that part of the North Shore.

When the unkind words became more than she could bear, Maud would sneak away, winter and summer, to comfort herself out among the trees. She would put her arms around their trunks, lean her head against them and shed the tears she was too proud to shed in front of her relatives. As it was with the Kings in *The Story Girl,* and the Murrays in the *Emily* books, it was a Macneill family custom to give the orchard trees names, sometimes for a newborn child, sometimes for the person who planted them, sometimes for something special about the tree. There was Uncle John's tree, Aunt Emily's tree, Uncle Leander's tree, Russell's tree, the little syrup tree, the spotty tree, the spider tree. Maud had more romantic names for the trees she loved best. The old maple and the spruce behind the barn that had grown so close together their branches entwined, she called The Lovers. The young birch in the corner by the stone dyke that fenced in the front garden was The White Lady, beloved of all the spicy, dark-green spruces that surrounded it.

She liked the farm animals and fowl—the chickens and turkeys, the sheep and the cows (although, when she was very small, she was afraid of the cows) but most of all, she loved the cats. She was, from her earliest days, like Sara Stanley, the *Story Girl,* "good friends with all cats." As Grandmother did not like cats, they lived in the barn and granary to keep the mice away so, when Maud was outside, she usually had at least one kitten in her apron pocket.

The outside was Maud's real world: the kitchen garden, the front garden that wasn't really a proper garden, but more of a little woodland because it was so full of trees and so overgrown with periwinkle, and the lacy white caraway and the blue-eyed grass that bloomed in the meadow beyond. The feeling she had for the natural world was more than love. She felt a part of it all—the green grass, the red earth, the snow on the bare tree branches outside her window in winter, the brook that always gurgled so happily in spring, the soughing wind and the sighing sea. She was a part of the shore—the rocks, the high sand dunes, and the tough marram grass that grew there. There was a kind of magic in all of it and she found that magic everywhere.

The narrow cow path that led from the Cavendish road to David and Margaret Macneill's house, through a silver-birch and evergreen wood, she called Lover's Lane, because it seemed so romantic with its sweet-scented wildflowers and the little log bridges over the shadowy brook. The dark wood below the hill field, she called The Haunted Wood, and the spot where the four oldest apple trees stood in the orchard, The Bower. She found a world for herself where there was balm for the wounds dealt her by the coldness of her grandparents and the unkindness of her aunts and uncles and cousins.

When Maud wrote of Jane Stuart, in *Jane of Lantern Hill*, "If you couldn't be loved, the next best thing was to be left alone," she must have written straight from her heart. She had only three real friends in those early years. One was her mother, in the only picture she had of her. It was a formal photograph of her in her best silk dress, with long jet earrings in her ears, her hair braided high on her head, and the stiff, proper expression on her face that a studio photograph in those days demanded. But there was a glimmer of humour at the corners of Clara Montgomery's mouth that she had not quite been able to hide— and she was lovely looking. Maud unburdened her poor, unloved, aching spirit to her mother-in-the-picture. She told her about the hurtful words, about her dreams, about how she wished she had curly hair, about the things that made her laugh that nobody else thought funny. She told her how she loved the trees and the brook and the wind. She told her stories. She called her mother her kindred spirit.

Her other two friends were Katie Maurice and Lucy Gray. Katie Maurice was a child like herself. Lucy Gray was a sad, grown-up widow who always had sad stories to tell. They were both reflections of herself that she'd found in the oval glass windows of the sitting-room bookcase and she saw them best—and liked them best—around twilight, when the fire was burning in the grate and the reflections were, "a glamour of light and shadow." She would whisper to these friends for as long as she was allowed to stand there, exchanging confidences with Katie Maurice, saying comforting words to Lucy Gray. Then she would leave them with a wave and a promise to return soon.

Out of this life among people who did not want her, before she could read or write or travel any great distance, this small child was creating what she called, when she was older, her "inward" life. It was a rich and marvellous life. It made her everyday "outward" life possible in its darkest moments and heightened its brightest ones. Already Maud had started building her house of dreams.

CHAPTER 2

Four Big Sweet Apples

"School was very different from what she had expected it to be, but that was the way in life, she had heard Ellen Greene say, and you just had to make the best of it."
—EMILY OF NEW MOON

On a warm spring day in 1881, when the sky was deep blue and the leaves were a pale lacy green on the trees, Maud skipped down the lane from her house. The chirping of chickadees and finches overhead seemed to echo the joy in her heart. Aunt Emily, walking sedately close behind, kept bidding her to slow down, but she couldn't. Her grey eyes shone with excitement in her small, thin face. Her gold-brown braids danced under her wide-brimmed felt hat. She had on her new wool dress with the starched white pinafore over it, her brown buttoned boots, polished to a high shine, and her best warm coat. Lucy Maud Montgomery was six-and-a-half years old and she was going to start school.

She did not have far to go. The school, a little one-room, white clapboard building, was just across the road from the gate at the foot of her own lane. As Aunt Emily opened the door and led her inside, everyone in the room looked up. Cousin Alec

Macneill waved at her and someone else whispered, "hello Maudie," but Maud felt the importance of the occasion too keenly to acknowledge anyone. She had been inside the school before for neighbourhood concerts, so the room itself, with its windows along the side walls, the wood stove between them, and the blackboard across the front, was familiar. But she'd never been there when the teacher's desk was at the front and the students' desks with their attached benches were set up in rows. And here they were, with children on all the benches, all with their eyes on her.

With a murmured, "Now, mind, you be a good girl," Aunt Emily departed. Mr. Ross, the teacher, sat Maud down at a desk near the back of the room beside two grade five girls, Cousin Pensie Macneill (Alec's older sister) and Pensie's friend Emma Stuart. He told them to look after her. They did. They petted her and fussed over her as though she were a prize kitten. With all that lovely attention, so much to listen to, so much to watch, so much to think about, Maud's day fairly flew by.

Eagerly she set out the next morning, all by herself this time and sure, now, that school was going to be every bit the wonderful adventure she had always imagined it would be. Carefully copying the other children, she hung her coat on the peg assigned to her in the porch, just inside the front door, and made her way to the bench where Pensie and Emma were sitting. From all around the room there were giggles and snorts of laughter.

"Maudie, you forgot to take off your hat," whispered Pensie. Maud was mortified. No one, no one at all, ever wore a hat indoors. She could feel the hot, red embarrassment flush her face. She snatched the hat from her head, lifted her chin in the air, marched out to the porch and hung it on the peg with her coat.

In the journal she started in her teens Maud wrote about that morning. "I felt that I was a target for the humiliation of the universe. Never, I felt certain, could I live down such a terrible mistake."

It didn't take Maud long to make sense out of the confusion of those first few days. She was squirming with impatience when Mr. Ross finally told her he thought she was ready to take her place with the children her own age and begin lessons. She was to share a desk and bench with Maud Woodside and the little girls were soon whispering and giggling together as comfortably as Pensie and her grade-five friends. All that spring the two Mauds were as close as two chicks in a nest.

In a one-room schoolhouse with over forty pupils in ten grades, the teacher could not spend much time in a day with each class. Mr. Ross would assign lessons to the classes he wasn't working with: reading, arithmetic sums, multiplication tables, spelling words or history lessons. But there were times when he would have spelling matches or out-loud reading for all ten grades at once. On one of those days, not long after Maud had arrived in school, he paid her a compliment.

It was during a reading practice. The children stood in rows beside their desks to read aloud in turn. Maud knew how to read. She had been entranced by words almost from the beginning of her life and, without really trying, she'd learned to read at the age of four. So, when her turn came, she stood beside her desk along the side aisle and read "How doth the little busy bee improve each shining hour" with great feeling, pronouncing each word loudly and clearly. Mr. Ross beamed his approval. Then he said to the whole room, "This little girl reads better than any of you, although she is younger and has never been to school before." It was the first compliment Maud could ever remember getting from anyone and she never forgot it. What a shock that sudden, unexpected praise was! Her heart was beating so loudly she was sure everyone in the room could hear it.

There were those in the class who did not think Maud's reading was so wonderful. The school was full of Macneill, Simpson and Clark cousins (as Maud wrote in her teen-age journal, "almost everybody in Cavendish who isn't a Simpson is a Macneill and mostly they are both."). Some of them had been tormenting Maud as long as she could remember. And there were others, not cousins, girls like Clara Mackenzie and Annie Stewart, who were envious of the neatly-dressed girl who wore polished buttoned boots when they went barefoot, and who was part of that Macneill family that thought so much of itself.

Those children took every chance they could to let Maud know they didn't think she was so fine. One of the girls told her that her pinafore was a baby apron and Maud hated that pinafore with a passion ever afterwards. She had to wear it, though. Grandmother Macneill refused to let her leave it off.

School never again held the promise of a great, unclouded adventure for her. She never forgot Mr. Ross's praise, but she never forgot the teasing or the mean words, either. The "Miss Pridey, Miss Pridey . . . you may have button boots, but you are living on charity," hissed across the schoolroom at Emily Starr, and Emily's "terrible gingham apron and equally terrible gingham sunbonnet," were described in *Emily of New Moon* by their author when she was past middle age and still felt the sting of those taunts.

But Maud was not one to display her wounds. She had too much steel in her makeup and she was too proud. Also, she had her own ways of hitting back. She had been the object of a sarcastic-tongued grandfather's "digs" all her young life and, like Emily, she was "quite able to give 'digs' herself . . . and she could give them with such merciless lucidity and irony that the others soon learned not to provoke them."

There was, too, something about Maud—a look in her eyes, a way of standing, a way of holding her head—that made people take notice, even when she was only six years old. There were those who resented her for it, but there were also those who were drawn to her because of it. And they were drawn to her because, like Sara Stanley in *The Story Girl,* "she was such a hand to tell stories." What's more, before the year was out, she was known, even by those who didn't like her, as one of the smartest children in the school. She liked school. She liked learning things and she liked her *Royal Reader* with its poems and stories.

Not all the boys teased, nor were all the girls spiteful. Maud made friends. Maud Woodside was always her devoted friend. The nice boy who lived up the road, Jack Laird, with his ready smile, was in her class. Cousin Alma Macneill, "with the dimpled cheeks and sweet smile," was one of Maud's favourites though her sister Clementine was not. Clemmie and her best friend Nellie Macneill (another distant cousin) were Maud's declared enemies almost from the day Maud began school. The Josie Pyes, the Jen Pringles, the Rhoda Stuarts—all the mean, spiteful girls in Maud's books—owe a lot to Clemmie and Nellie for the vividness of their characters. And how the grown-up Maud must have enjoyed putting them there!

On the other hand, there was Cousin Pensie. She was four years older than Maud and she was kind, someone to rely on and confide in. Then, after the spring term, there was Amanda.

Amanda was one of Cousin William Macneill's six children and lived out in the country beyond the village. She started school in the summer, a few months after Maud (school had no long summer holidays in those years, so the new term began in June). For the first two days Amanda was petted and fussed over by Pensie and Emma as Maud had been. Maud loved Amanda dearly and she wanted to share her desk and bench with her. So, shamelessly, she bought the privilege of Amanda's company from Pensie with "four big, sweet apples" from Grandfather Macneill's prized orchard. Many years later, she wrote in her journal, "It was not a bad bargain for four apples!!!" The two girls became "bosom friends." They played together during the "dinner recess" and after school and they sat beside each other for the rest of their school years.

Recess. The grown-up Maud wrote in her journal, "I will always be thankful that my school was near a grove—a spruce grove with winding paths and treasure trove of ferns and mosses and violets . . . and there was a brook in it, too—a delightful brook with a big, deep clear spring where we went for buckets of water."

They picked the gum from the spruce trees to chew, waded in the brook in warm weather, and while the boys played tag or a ball game in the schoolyard, the girls made playhouses among the trees. Rain or shine, two or three girls together would find a little glade formed by clusters of bushes, a grove of trees, or a spot flattened by deer or raccoons. There they would make seats of stones, cupboards of clumps of moss, and put in them bits of broken plates and cups they'd found at home. They competed furiously for whose was the best—it was usually Maud's—until some recesses would break up in tears and screams and even hair-pulling. Others would end in happy exchanges of ideas until it got so late that all that could be heard of the teacher's back-to-class bell was its echo.

And so, even before that first year was over, the odour of chalk mingled with the wood smoke from the stove and the drying wool from skirts and breeches that had got wet in the brook, the sight and the scent of the spruce grove through the window, were familiar and comfortable. Maud felt that the schoolroom and the children in it were as much home and family as the big house up the lane with Aunt Emily and the two old people who lived there.

CHAPTER 3

Happy Times at Park Corner

"There, among sibilant spruces and firs, was the old, whitewashed house—from which presently a light gleamed through an open door . . ."—THE STORY GIRL

Every summer before she was old enough to go to school Maud went to Park Corner to visit her Montgomery relatives. She always looked forward to that visit for months. The summer before she was six, her father came home from one of his far-away jobs to drive her from Cavendish and her happiness was complete.

Even though Park Corner was only a little over twenty kilometres from Cavendish, it was almost a whole days' journey in the horse-drawn buggy. They set off early in the morning. The day was warm, cloudless and sunny. With her small hand in his big one, Maud told her father everything that was going on in her world. Most of it was about starting school in the fall and what a "scrumptious adventure" it was going to be. Bouncing up and down on the buggy seat, turning her head to look this way and that, she chattered on as the horse trotted along the dusty red road. Up and down the hills they went, through woods, over two rivers and along the shore. They stopped by a brook under a big elm tree so the horse could have a drink and they could eat the lunch Grandmother had packed for them.

It was a perfect drive except for having to go on the drawbridges over the rivers. Maud was terrified of them. She held her breath until her face turned red and squeezed Father's hand as hard as she could when the horse stepped on "the draw" because she was sure it was going to spring open at the exact moment he put his hoof on it. It didn't—it never did—and, as soon as the buggy was safely over, she breathed a big sigh. It wasn't long, then, before they were in Park Corner, driving up to the big white house, and there were Grandfather and Grandmother Montgomery coming through the front door to greet them.

In her journal, a long time later, Maud wrote that Grandfather Montgomery was, "a dear, lovable . . . handsome old man . . . just like a grandfather out of a story book." He was a big, broad-shouldered man, beardless and grey-haired, with dark blue eyes and stern features that would often relax into the gentlest of smiles. Grandmother Montgomery was Grandfather's second wife. She didn't take much interest in her stepchildren or in their children. Maud remembered her later as a rather vain woman who wore elaborate caps on her head and who kept to herself in her own sitting room much of the time, where she read or sewed or entertained her friends.

The Montgomery house was often full of Montgomery relatives—Uncle Jim and Uncle Cuthbert, who still lived at home when Maud was very small, Aunt Maggie Sutherland and Aunt Mary McIntyre, visiting from Charlottetown, sometimes with their husbands and children, Aunt Jane and Uncle Charles Crosby and their children, who lived nearby, and often some of the Campbells from across the road. It was a comfortable old frame house with two gables and a porch along one end. It had been built in bits over many years, so that it fit together awkwardly in places and "was full of cupboards and nooks, and little, unexpected flights of stairs." There was a big grandfather clock in the front hall and in the downstairs sitting room on the mantel there was a pair of white china dogs with green spots. Maud's father told her once that, whenever the dogs heard the grandfather clock strike midnight, they jumped down from the mantel and barked.

Through all her youngest years, Maud begged to be allowed to stay up to watch and listen to this amazing performance, but she was never allowed up that late. One day, one of her cousins told her that it wasn't true, that she had been in that sitting room at midnight and the dogs hadn't moved, hadn't made a sound. Maud was outraged. Her father had lied to her! When she confronted him, he told her very solemnly that the reason those particular dogs did not bark at midnight had to be because they were china and couldn't hear the clock strike. Maud could understand that and she forgave him but for years she secretly clung to the hope that one day they really might bark. (Even after she grew up, she still loved those china dogs. She gave them to Patty's Place in *Anne of the Island,* complete with their green spots, and then moved them to Anne's own house in *Anne's House of Dreams*).

Uncle John and Aunt Annie Campbell's house across the road was also big and white, but it was newer than Maud's grandparents' house. On the gable over its front door, it had beautiful "gingerbread" trim wound about with honeysuckle that smelled wonderful, and all around the house were apple orchards—the trees always with little shiny green apples on them in summer, the only time of year Maud was there when she was a child. The house stood on a rise above a large sparkling pond that held such magic for her that she gave it to Avonlea when she wrote *Anne of Green Gables* and called it "The Lake of Shining Waters." Behind was "a grove of fir and spruce, a dim, cool place where the winds were fond of purring and where there was always a resinous, woodsy odour." Maud wrote that in *The Story Girl* about the King farm, but she was really describing the Campbell farm in Park Corner.

Maud loved Aunt Annie and Uncle John with all her heart. Aunt Annie never called her sly or impertinent as Aunt Ann Maria did. She did not scold as Aunt Emily did. She always seemed to have time for Maud as Grandmother Macneill did not. And Uncle John was kind and jolly. The Campbell house echoed with his booming laughter, the sound of Aunt Annie bustling about and the happy noise of Maud's three oldest Campbell cousins, George, Stella and Clara, running and shouting in the halls—Frederica (Frede), the youngest, was born when Maud was seven.

That house was always filled with the aroma of good cooking and Aunt Annie's baking—bread, cake, berry pie. And there were even more people coming or going from there than from Grandfather Montgomery's house. There would be Montgomery and Crosby and Campbell uncles and aunts, with neighbours and friends from nearby French River. Maud was so happy in that house she could barely contain herself. Sometimes she would just stand inside the front door and stare at everything that was going on. Sometimes she would rush right in and tear through the halls after her cousins. At dinner she would sit in her chair at the long dining room table, silent as a ghost, watching, listening, carefully storing away in her mind the laughter and the good-natured talk and Uncle John presiding at the head, "carving up platters of geese and turkeys."

She fished in the pond with her cousins, romped through the evergreen groves behind the house, played dress-up and make-believe in the attic, and went home to Cavendish every year with a head full of good memories—except for that summer just before she was six.

One evening towards the end of that visit, she was in her grandparents' kitchen, standing on tip-toe by the stove watching the cook stir up the fire with the iron poker. She loved to stir it up herself and watch "the glowing red embers fall down on the black ashes" so, as soon as the cook put the poker down, Maud grabbed it—by the red-hot end that had been in the fire. Instantly she dropped it and let out a shrill scream. The pain was excruciating.

At once everyone came running. The cook went into hysterics. Grandfather shouted at the cook. Father begged someone to do something. Grandmother grabbed the bucket of water from the cupboard. One of the maids, thinking it would help, shoved Maud's hand into a saucer of kerosene. A new more horrible pain shot up her arm. She screamed louder and someone yanked the kerosene away. Father pulled Maud onto his lap and thrust her hand into the bucket of cold water. It was the only thing that eased the pain even the slightest bit and Maud finally cried herself to sleep cradled in Father's arms with her hand up to the elbow in the bucket of water.

She remembered that night always, the pain of the burn, the smell and the feel of the awful kerosene, the bucket of water—and the attention she was getting. Being the centre of all that attention was not something she was used to and it was a great thing to remember, in spite of the pain.

She woke the next morning with her hand still throbbing and a miserable headache. Father hugged her gently, helped her into her dress and her pinafore and joked a little to try to cheer her up. He carried her to the breakfast table. Cook brought in the porridge but Maud's headache was worse and she was feeling sicker by the minute. The porridge looked like pig slop, the milk like dish water. She began to cry. Father picked her up again and, with Grandmother's help, undressed her and put her to bed in a little room off the sitting room.

To everyone's horror, it turned out that her sick headache had nothing to do with the burn on her hand. She had typhoid fever. Typhoid fever was so dangerous and so contagious that no one else was allowed into the house but the doctor and Grandmother Macneill who came from Cavendish to help nurse. Maud almost died. She lay for over a month in that little room with the curtains tightly drawn. Her fever was so high she was delirious. She didn't recognise Grandmother Macneill. She thought she was a dreadful old woman named Mrs Murphy and she screamed every time Grandmother came near. It was some time before her fever subsided. When it finally did and she was no longer delirious she realized that the woman sitting on the chair beside her bed was her grandmother. She was overjoyed. She stroked her grandmother's face lovingly. "You are *not* Mrs. Murphy after all—you are Grandma," she cried and would not let her leave her side.

It was months before she was completely well again. Furthermore, in those days, doctors insisted that people who'd had serious illnesses like typhoid fever needed a long, quiet time to convalesce, so Maud was bundled into the buggy, wrapped in blankets and furs against the late summer breezes, and taken home to Cavendish to be kept quiet all winter. Her dream of going to school—the scrumptious adventure—was not to be met that fall. She was six and a half years old when the adventure began the next spring.

CHAPTER 4

Books, Boats, Brothers and Bosom Friends

"Ours had been the little, loving tasks of every day, blithe companionship, shared thoughts, and adventuring."
—THE STORY GIRL

Once Maud was in school, she could no longer have those leisurely summer visits to Park Corner. She missed them, but summer in Cavendish was too busy for her to wish for long to be somewhere else. There were frequent visits from her father: he would go walking with her or take her out driving. She had school and Sunday-school lessons. She had her chores to do: dusting, drying dishes, weeding the garden, feeding the chickens and turkeys and leading the sheep and cows to pasture. As she grew she helped with butter churning and cheese making too.

In the days when Maud was a child, mackerel were plentiful in the sea around the Island. Starting in early spring, most of the Cavendish farmers anchored fishing boats just off shore and threw their nets over the side. Grandfather kept a boat but, because he was old, he hired others to fish for him. The men would go out before dawn, then the children would be sent down at eight o'clock with their breakfasts. They'd be sent again at noon with dinner and, if the fish were still "schooled" all afternoon, again with supper. Maud always went with Prescott and Lucy, the two of Uncle John's children nearest her own age. Together they carried the baskets full of bread and butter, cheese, hard-cooked eggs, cold meat and pie and, at noon time, the plates of hot dinner, wrapped in tea towels.

"The Cavendish shore is a very beautiful one," Maud said in *The Alpine Path,* a book of memories she wrote long after she was a published author, "part of it is rock shore, where the rugged red cliffs rise steeply from the boulder-strewn coves. Part is a long, gleaming sand shore, divided from the fields and ponds behind by a row of rounded sand dunes, covered by coarse sand-hill grass." During the brief school breaks, when it wasn't raining (and, sometimes, when it was) most of the children in Cavendish would be on the beach all day, splashing about in the sea, gathering shells and stones, eating mussels and dulse "by the yard."

Maud was very sociable. She revelled in the company of other children and more often than not led in the games of "ball, knifey, Stepstone, or King, King, Come along." But she also needed a lot of time to herself. She needed to tell her dolls their stories and give them their tea from their tiny china tea set and tuck them into the doll bed her father had given them. She needed time for Katie Maurice and Lucy Gray. She needed time to lie in the tall grass, to breathe in the mingled fragrance of caraway and clover and watch the little blue and yellow butterflies. She needed to sit on the back step with the cats. Even though Grandmother hated cats and wouldn't have one in the house, there were always lots of cats in the barn and the granary to keep the rats and mice away. Maud gave them all names and she loved every one of them. Wherever she went, outside the house, there would be a cat with her, cuddled up against her neck, peering out from the pocket of her pinafore, following at her heels. But most of all, she needed time to read.

As soon as she had learned to read the simple stories in the first *Royal Reader,* at the age of four, Maud gave herself up to the lure of literature. When she was older she would talk about having "book sprees" and being "drunk on books," but, in those early years, she only knew that books transported her to as magical a realm as the woods and meadows did. The stories in books were different from the stories she listened to, much as she loved those. A book story could be read over and over, savoured, have dreams woven around it, and be kept to oneself for as long as one wished, like a precious secret. One day Maud stood in front of Grandfather's bookshelves in the parlour and made up her mind that she would read every book on them.

There weren't all that many, even though Grandfather, himself, loved to read. He took a daily newspaper from Charlottetown and Grandmother had her *Godey's Lady's Book* magazine full of stories, poems, and fashion drawings. There was the big family Bible. There was *The Pilgrim's Progress*—in those days, in every Christian household where there were books, there was a copy of John Bunyan's inspirational allegory. There were other Christian books and missionary tracts, two volumes of *The History of the World,* a few novels for adults, and one story for children titled *Little Katey and Jolly Jim.*

Grandfather read the Bible aloud every night after supper,

seated at the big table in the sitting room, summer and winter, and, afterwards, Maud was allowed to sit at the kitchen table with the light from the oil lamp shining on the book and read again the stories that gripped her. She would roll the lovely, long, exotic words and beautiful phrases around on her tongue. Then she would close the big book and go off murmuring to herself, " a firmament in the midst of the waters," or, "Hew thee two tables of stone . . ." or names like Ahasueras and Vashti and Absalom and Nebuchadnezzar.

In time, she did read every book on Grandfather's shelves, but not during the summer she was six and a half, and she was well into her teens before she had any wish to read most of the novels or *The Pilgrim's Progress*. But she spent many a blissful evening poring over the fashion drawings in the *Godey's Lady's Book*. She imagined herself grown up, resplendent in the elegant silk, bustled gowns, her hair curled and pinned up under one of the "exquisite" hats covered with chiffon and feathers. While she didn't exactly pore over the missionary tracts, she was fascinated by "their bizarre drawings of cannibal chiefs." The one book she read over and over was *Little Katey and Jolly Jim,* because it was about children and not too full of moral lessons. She thought it was "simply scrumptious."

Summer passed. Fall came. Maud turned seven in November and that winter Aunt Emily was married. For weeks the household prepared for the wedding. Grandmother spent all her time in the kitchen with aunts and cousins, churning butter and baking, not only wedding cake, but all sorts of other delicious cakes and pies, both sweet and savoury. Laughing, gossiping, humming as they worked, the busy cooks roasted, baked and boiled hams, chickens and turkeys (hams, chickens and turkeys Maud had watched being slaughtered out behind the barn), set jellies and baked breads. There wasn't a bare table-top or a cupboard shelf in either the kitchen or the summer cook house just outside the kitchen door. What glorious odours wafted through that old farm house!

In the sitting room dressmakers were hard at work making Aunt Emily's trousseau. Maud would slide herself into the little cane-bottomed chair in the corner behind the door and soak up every single detail. First the cloth would be cut out on the big oval table. Then it would be pinned and basted and Aunt Emily would be fitted. Then out would come the thimbles and the needles and thread and, in no time at all, petticoats, waists, skirts and gowns would appear. The wedding gown was Maud's favourite. It was brown silk with "pleatings and flounces." It swept the floor with its train and it rustled when Aunt Emily moved—and it had a bustle just like the gowns in the *Godey's Lady's Book*.

Then Maud, herself, had to be fitted for a new dress. Not silk. Little girls in Cavendish, Prince Edward Island in 1881 did not have silk dresses. In fact, most grown women were lucky to own one silk dress in a lifetime. Maud's dress was a plain, dark wool with a white lace collar, but she was not going to have to wear a pinafore over it and she was going to be allowed to have her long hair, if not curled, at least un-braided.

The wedding was everything a wedding should be. Friends and neighbours came from many kilometres away—and so did relatives on both sides of Maud's family, because her new uncle, John Montgomery, was her father's first cousin. They came in their best silks and their fine suits and they filled the Presbyterian church for the ceremony at seven o'clock in the evening. When it was over, they all got into their carriages and buggies and drove back to the house, where candles and lamps were lit throughout and fires burned brightly in every room. Piled in bowls and heaped on platters, the sumptuous feast that had been so long in preparation was served on Grandmother's best flowered china dishes in the dining room.

Aunt Emily looked lovely in her brown silk gown, her pretty face shining under a jet-black bonnet with a white feather. Cousin Grace Macneill, her bridesmaid, also had a brown silk dress, not as grand as the bride's but, to Maud's eyes, very fine indeed. Aunt Emily's new husband, Uncle John Montgomery, was handsome in his dark suit, high white starched collar and dark tie.

Uncle John was a kind, warm-hearted man with a laugh as loud and jolly as Uncle John Campbell's and Maud liked him very much, but, suddenly, when she saw him standing beside Aunt Emily being congratulated by all those people, she hated him. He was taking Aunt Emily away. Life would change— and Maud hated the uncertainty of change. She flew at him with both fists flying and screamed at him not to take Aunt Emily away. Some of the guests laughed. Some of them scolded. Uncle John just picked her up and comforted her and she loved him forever after.

After supper the music began in the parlour. Someone played the piano. Several men had brought their fiddles. The furniture was pushed back against the walls, the rug was rolled up. To the tunes of Scottish reels and jigs, men and women lined up opposite one another and the dancing began. Then, when the dancers were tired out, everyone urged the best singers to perform—and there were games, games for the children, games for the adults. By this time, Maud had recovered from her outburst of grief and, her eyes shining with the excitement of it all, she played blind man's buff and drop the handkerchief with Amanda and Pensie and Lucy and the Crosby and Campbell children until way after midnight. Then, before it was time for everyone to leave, Grandmother and the aunts brought out a late supper.

The occasion was so unusual that Maud never forgot it. The Macneills did not celebrate birthdays. In *Emily of New Moon* Aunt Elizabeth tells Emily that "birthday parties were all nonsense . . ." Likely that's what Grandmother Macneill thought about them. And Christmas was strictly a religious occasion. Maud's description of that wedding ends on a wistful note, "Aunt Emily's wedding was the last festivity in this old house. With her went all the social life that had ever centred here. Grandfather and Grandmother were left to settle into the indifferent routine of age and I to grow up in that routine."

Even though there were no more parties and the old couple never again entertained anybody but family, other people still came to the post office every day. And, while Grandmother did not encourage Maud to invite her friends home, she gave permission for Pensie and Amanda and Lucy to come once in a while. She allowed Maud to go to their houses, too, after school and occasionally overnight.

Maud never went home overnight to Lucy's. Uncle John and Aunt Ann Maria were not very welcoming and the boys teased too much. It was great fun to go home with Amanda but even more fun to go home with Pensie. Pensie, herself, was full of fun, her dark eyes always alight with laughter. What's more, her whole family was lively. She had six brothers and sisters and theirs was, like Aunt Annie and Uncle John Campbell's in Park Corner, a cheerful house where something was always going on.

Maud badly needed a cheerful place to go that summer. Her father had decided to go out to the Northwest Territories. The Canadian Pacific Railway was just being built through the prairies and the Canadian government was encouraging settlement there. Maud was inconsolable. The morning he left she clung like a burr to him, sobbing heartbrokenly. The Northwest Territories were thousands of kilometres away. She was sure she would never see him again. The anguish she felt about his leaving imbedded itself deep in her spirit. When she was grown up and writing books, she relived it over and over again, feeling it anew each time, fresh and sharp, in stories about her orphans, Anne Shirley and Emily Starr, and with Jane Stuart in *Jane of Lantern Hill*.

Then something almost miraculous happened. Not long after Maud's father left, two orphan boys, Wellington and David Nelson, came to live at the Macneill house. What a glorious turn of events that was! It was almost like having brothers. And they were nice brothers. Wellington, who was called Well, was Maud's age. Dave was a year younger. They were a good-looking pair of boys. Well had dark-hair and eyes and a "merry face." Dave was "fair and blue-eyed." They were as different in interests as in looks. Well was studious while Dave was "a born mechanic, never happier than when tinkering away with scraps of old iron and wood." The only characteristic they seemed to share was a hot temper.

They never turned it on Maud and she soon got over being worried that they might. But she never got over being astonished by the way they went at each other—and how often. One evening late that autumn, Grandmother went out to the wedding of Cousin Grace Macneill (who had been Aunt Emily's bridesmaid). Aunt Emily and Aunt Annie Campbell came from Park Corner for the wedding and Aunt Annie brought Clara with her to keep Maud company. Grandfather stayed home to look after the children. Usually, when Well and Dave began to fight, Grandfather put an end to it with one barked order, but, on this evening, maybe because he was feeling pleased with himself that he had managed to stay home from the wedding, he told them to go ahead and punch each other all night if they wanted to.

They did want to. For two whole hours they rolled around on the kitchen floor, their faces "rooster" red, the sounds of their punches, kicks, howls and grunts coming through two walls into Maud's bedroom off the sitting room where she and Clara "played calmly, safe from the racket and the din . . ." At ten o'clock sharp Grandfather said "Enough!" and sent all the children to bed. Well and Dave "were black and blue for a week" but they told Maud they'd loved every minute of it. Her eyes still wide with amazement, Maud said, "I guess you wish Grace Macneill would get married every day."

That Grandfather-approved fight was a one-time-only event. Most evenings that fall and winter, the three children sat around the kitchen table and there could be no arguments, no fighting with Grandmother sitting nearby in her chair, knitting or mending. All that could be heard was the wind outside, the occasional crackle from the wood burning in the stove, and the sound of their subdued voices as they did their homework and their Sunday-school lessons. They played dominoes, tic-tac-toe, keep your temper, and other games; they read the *Wide Awake* magazines the boys' aunt sent them for a while—the last installment of a serial Maud was reading was due when the magazine stopped coming. The boys thought this was a huge joke. Maud finished it for herself, but she wasn't at all satisfied with what she'd written and she swore she'd never in her life read another magazine serial (thirty years later she came across bound copies of *Wide Awake* and was finally able to finish reading that story).

They told ghost stories. In school Well won the teacher's prize for being the best in arithmetic that winter, a copy of Hans Andersen's *Fairy Tales*. Maud was enchanted by the book. Then she won a collection of fairy tales for being top student most often and it had a story in it called *The Honey Stew of the Countess Bertha* which "abounded in ghosts" and she liked it even better. She loved "the cold chills" that ran up and down her spine but the stories scared her so much that she was always terrified to go to bed afterwards. She would rush through her prayers, dive under the covers and pull them over her head. Then she would lie awake for the longest time while her imagination went to work and the stories grew more horrifying by the minute.

The second summer the Nelson boys lived in Cavendish, the summer of 1883, the great *Marco Polo,* now old but once the fastest clipper ship to sail the seas, ran ashore on Cape Cavendish, not two kilometres from the Macneill gate.

There was a raging wind coming in from the sea that day. It hurled black waves high up onto the sand, it whistled and moaned and whipped the trees around up on the clifftops and through the farmyards. There were no fishing

boats out that day but someone living near the shore spot-
ted the clipper's sails and the news ran round the village
faster than the wind that a sailing ship was in trouble and
headed their way fast.

School was in session, so Maud did not see the ship come
in (and lamented that fact ever after). Everyone who could get
to the beach was there. What a sight it was! There, ploughing
through the heaving, pitching waves, was that great black clipper ship racing for the shore "straight on before the northern
gale with every stitch of canvas set," Maud wrote in her journal a few years later. She got the description from the people
who saw it happen. "She grounded about three hundred yards
from the shore and as she struck the crew cut the rigging, and
the huge masts went over with a crash that was heard for a
mile, above the roaring of the storm."

It was another whole day before the storm abated enough
for the crew to get to shore. There were twenty of them:
Irishmen, Englishmen, Scotsmen, Spaniards, Norwegians,
Swedes, Dutchmen, Germans and two Tahitians. They were
boarded out in homes around Cavendish, where nobody had
ever seen so many foreigners. The English, the Scots, and the
Irish didn't seem so strange, nor did the other Europeans,
despite their mysterious languages, but the two dark-skinned
Tahitians seemed wonderfully exotic in this little Scots-
Canadian community.

The sailors were obliged to stay put for several weeks
because there was so much official business to be done before
they could be paid. The Norwegian captain was boarding at
Maud's house, so the crew members were often there and
Maud and Well and Dave were the envy of every child in

Cavendish. They even got to watch "with eyes as big as owls" when, finally, with all the official business over and done with, the captain covered the round table in the parlour with gold sovereigns to pay off his crew. "Never," said Maud, "had we imagined there was so much wealth in the world."

A few weeks later there was a "wreck sale," an auction of the ship's hull and fittings and all its cargo, held in Grandfather's barn. People came from all over the Island: businessmen, auctioneers, souvenir hunters and just onlookers like Maud and Well and Dave who not only watched but eagerly bit into the dry, tasteless ship's biscuits that were piled up on the barn floor for everyone to try.

Seven years later, when she was in grade ten, Maud came third among the Island's Queen's County students in a Canada-wide school composition contest with her entry: *The Wreck of the Marco Polo*.

Summers were not always as exciting as the summer the *Marco Polo* came aground on the Cavendish shore but Maud and Well and Dave always had good times together. They built playhouses and swings. They swam in the sea. They sat in the barn or out in the woods while Maud told stories (as Sara Stanley did in *The Story Girl*). They "ranged happily through the fields and orchards in the beautiful summer twilights." They fished for trout from the log bridges in Lovers' Lane and in "the Birch Pool under the roots of an overhanging clump of white birches in a woodsy corner." Maud hated to put the worm on the hook but she did it because she couldn't bear to have the boys think she wasn't brave. One day she not only put her own worm on the hook, she caught the biggest trout. She figured she had gone up "ten percent" in the boys' estimation.

When Uncle Leander's family came for their vacation, Fred, who was near in age, had to be included in their play— Murray, who was older and thought quite a lot of himself, wouldn't be seen in their company and the others were still very small. Sometimes they were obliged to include Uncle's John's kids. Prescott was with them the day Maud caught the big trout and it impressed him so much he never again looked on her with quite so much disdain.

For three years the Nelson brothers lived in Cavendish. Before they left, Well gave Maud a miniature china dog he treasured. She was thrilled by the gift. She kept it on her dresser top and, when she was older and went away to school or work, the dog always went with her. She missed the boys sorely when they left. When she wrote *The Story Girl*, which she always said was her favourite book, Well and Dave Nelson became Felix and Bev King. She set that story in Park Corner, but many of the adventures—including the ghostly bell that turned out to be a long-silent old clock—were things that really happened in Cavendish with Well and Dave.

It wasn't easy to settle down to being an only child again. But Maud had her cats, she had her Haunted Wood and her Lovers Lane, she had her books and, like the heroine of one of the magazine stories she wrote when she was grown up, she was "never lonely when she was alone." She simply moved into her imaginary world.

CHAPTER 5

To Be a Writer

*. . . and then she poured out her tale of the day—of her rapture and her pain—writing heedlessly and intently until the sunset faded into dim, star-litten twilight . . . Emily, in the throes of literary composition, was lost to all worldly things.—*EMILY OF NEW MOON

"I am going to begin a new kind of diary," Maud wrote when she was fourteen years old. "I have kept one of a kind . . . ever since I was a tot of nine. But I burned it today. It was so silly I was ashamed of it. And it was also very dull."

It probably wasn't at all dull, or silly. Maud began it right after she had read a book called *A Bad Boy's Diry*, a story a teacher had left behind in the house after boarding there for a year. It was meant to be funny and it was written as though by "little Gorgie," a mischievous boy who couldn't spell. Maud thought the book was so good she "folded and cut and sewed four sheets of foolscap into a book and covered it with red paper." She wrote *Maud Montgomery's Diry* on the red-paper cover and made up naughty tricks to write about and spelled them badly on purpose (although she couldn't spell very well, anyway). The "diry" didn't last long as an account of naughty tricks because Maud wasn't very interested in mischief. Her "diry" was soon full of thoughts about trees and flowers, her observations about people and daily events.

By the age of nine she was already writing furiously on any stray bits of paper she could find. In this she had a friend in her grandfather. Grandfather Macneill was a constant reader and a man who wrote well himself—although he never tried to publish anything. When he noticed that Maud was spending so much time writing, he saw to it that she had paper. Since he ran the post office, there were always government letter bills— red postal forms that were "half a yard long" and printed on one side only. They came three times a week with the mail and were always thrown out after they were checked over. There were also little yellow notebooks that Dr. Pierce's patent-medicine firm sent out as advertising.

Hungrily, Maud snatched these up. She wrote her "diry" in the notebooks and, like Emily Starr, her stories and poems on the backs of the letter bills. She wrote in every spare moment, squirrelling away every last stub of pencil she found, feverishly putting on paper the poems that came to her out in the orchard or woods, jotting down every story idea, every new, interesting word, every description of a person or place. Writing, for Maud, was not just a pleasure, it was as necessary as breathing. It was almost a spiritual exercise. It filled her soul. Maud, like Emily, when "in the delightful throes of literary composition, was lost to all worldly things" and the cows went unfetched, the chickens unfed, and the cats didn't get their saucers of milk. Without ever making a conscious decision, she knew she was going to be a writer when she grew up.

Her stories, in those days, weren't stories about herself or people she knew. They were dark melodramas about noble prisoners being beheaded or burned at the stake. She had found a book about the Tower of London in her Park Corner grand-parents' house. She was horrified by the executions but she was also fascinated and she had to create her own hair-raising tales. Sometimes her stories were about battles, sometimes, after she read *Ivanhoe,* they were about murder and revenge and broken-hearted heroines dressed in silks and satins and glittering jewels. A great number of them were pious tales inspired by a book she read on Sundays when she was only allowed to read religious works. She loved that book.

It was called *The Memoir of Anzonetta Peters* and it was the story of a child who became ill at the age of five, turned to religion, and lived a saintly life until she died when she was twelve. Anzonetta talked only in hymns. For months Maud's life was taken over by this book. She tried valiantly to become as saintly as her idol, although she didn't try to talk in hymns—she knew how she would be laughed at for that. She failed miserably at behaviour even approaching Anzonetta's but she did write hymns in her diary and she wrote a lot of Anzonetta-like stories. The longest of them was a tragedy about an immigrant preacher's wife whose children died, one by one, as their mother crossed Canada from Newfoundland to British Columbia. It was called *The Graves* and, in it, Maud described, with doleful realism, each death-bed and each grave-side scene. She gave it to Anne Shirley for one of the childhood stories Anne remembered in *Anne of the Island.*

Stories about dead and dying people came partly from Maud's keen sense of drama and her ever-inventive imagination. They came partly from living at a time when illnesses like pneumonia, influenza and measles regularly carried off neighbours and schoolmates. They came from the tuberculosis that had killed her mother and the typhoid fever that had almost taken her own life. Some of them must have been written out of the pain she felt about a barnyard tragedy that took place one summer morning not long after she had begun keeping her "diry."

That year she had two kittens she particularly loved, Catkin and Pussy-willow, named for cats in the *Wide Awake* magazine. She had locked them in the granary to save them from Gyp, the dog, whose "one very bad fault," was that he "hated cats and pursued them to the death." Pussy-willow was a grey-striped kitten; he was bouncy and bold and he was her favourite. Early one summer morning she raced out to the granary before school to see them and she found Pussy-willow writhing on the floor in agony. He had eaten part of a poisoned rat. With a cry, Maud dropped to the floor and pulled the kitten into her arms. She stroked him, she cuddled him, she whispered his name over and over but there wasn't anything she could do. In the bright morning sunlight, she had to watch with horror as he grew "stiff and cold" before her eyes. Suddenly she grasped the sharp reality of death as she never had with the death of people she had known or even at the sight of a dead body in a coffin. She saw the life leave that kitten and she understood completely that, from that moment, Pussy-willow would never again be anything but a scrap of dead, grey fur. She cried until there were no more tears left to cry with.

After that morning, the mournful stories Maud wrote on the backs of the letter bills had a depth of feeling in them that pious books like *The Memoir of Anzonetta Peters* could not match. But it wasn't all tragedy for the budding author's busy pencil. She wrote biographies of cats, past and present, and of dolls. She wrote flowery descriptions of Lovers' Lane, the Bower, the Haunted Wood, and the sea. She wrote her first poem after reading *Seasons,* a book of poems by James Thomson, written in blank verse. Maud was so enraptured by them that she had to sit down at once to write one of her own. It was called *Autumn.* In *Emily of New Moon,* Emily has that same book and writes that same poem.

> "Now autumn comes, laden with peach and pear;
> The sportsman's horn is heard throughout the land,
> And the poor partridge, fluttering, falls dead."

In spite of faithfully modelling her poem after Mr. Thomson's, complete with his hunter and horn, Maud's heart was with "the poor partridge." The poem itself met almost as sad a fate as the bird (as did Emily's poem). Maud's father was home for a rare visit from the Northwest Territories that year and he came to Cavendish to see her on "the very day" she wrote it. Proudly she brought it out to show him, just as Emily showed hers to Aunt Laura.

"It doesn't sound much like poetry, Maudie," he said doubtfully (as Aunt Laura said to Emily).

"It's blank verse," she cried.

"Very blank indeed." (As Aunt Laura said, too) He handed it back to her, smiling.

Maud was crushed (as was Emily). She did not show him another scrap of her writing and, after that, she wrote all her poetry in rhyme. Furthermore she hid the poem—and everything else she had ever written—in two shelf-like spaces formed by the boards that had been nailed to the bottom of each end of the sitting-room sofa. No scornful eyes would ever uncover her precious manuscripts there.

There were more poems, more stories, more biographies stuffed into those shelves under the sofa every week and every month as the years went on. Maud wrote lyrically about the stars and the moon, the sun and the sea, the brook and the Haunted Wood. One she called *The Tree Lovers* was about the old maple and spruce behind the barn with their entwined branches. In the poem, when the maple died, the spruce "held her dead form in his green, faithful arms" until finally he, too, died. Another, *The Monarch of the Forest*, was about a tree Maud thought of as her "tree of trees," a huge old birch that stood at the edge of the Haunted Wood.

"Around the poplar and the spruce
The fir and maple stood;
But the old tree that I loved the best
Grew in the Haunted Wood."

She did not show that poem to anyone. The next time she looked for approval of her writing, she was twelve, three years older than when she showed her father *Autumn*—and much wiser. It was when her teacher, Miss Izzy Robinson, was boarding at her house. Grandfather disliked Miss Robinson and went to great pains to let her know it with his digs and bars. Miss Robinson took out her feelings about Grandfather on Maud in school. She was viciously sarcastic to her and she gave her as little credit as possible for the work she did. Maud was sure that, if she were to show her the poem she had written, Miss Robinson would shoot it down with a poisoned arrow. But she badly wanted the teacher's opinion. So she approached her with a ruse one summer evening at home in the kitchen after supper, while Miss Robinson was sitting at the table, sewing.

Because Miss Robinson liked songs and was quite a good singer, Maud asked her, "Have you ever heard a song called *Evening Dreams?*"

"I don't recall a song by that title," Miss Robinson answered stiffly, "Do you know its words?" whereupon Maud recited the poem in such a tremulous voice and ended on such a gasp she was sure the teacher would guess the poem was her own.

Miss Robinson had her attention on her sewing and didn't notice Maud's nervousness. "I don't know it,"she said, "but the words are very pretty." Maud excused herself somehow. She sailed out into "the amber air of the summer evening and danced down the lane under the birches in a frenzy of delight," but, even in that rapturous moment, she thought it was hilarious that Izzy Robinson, who would have swallowed her tongue before she would wittingly praise Maud Montgomery, had told her the words of her poem were "very pretty."

That praise meant so much to Maud that, the following winter, she copied *Evening Dreams* in ink in her very best handwriting and sent it to the editor of one of the magazines that came to her grandmother. Alas, the editor of the magazine did not share Miss Robinson's opinion. He sent the poem back without comment. Poor Maud! How she suffered the pain of that rejection! She was not one to give up on anything, however—not for ever. A year later she copied the poem out again and sent it to a newspaper in Charlottetown. For two intoxicating weeks she dreamed of herself as a published poet, basking in the approval of her grandfather, the envy of all her schoolmates, a Cavendish celebrity. It was not to be. The paper never printed the poem and the editor did not even send it back to Maud. She was in "the depths of despair." She threw *Evening Dreams* into the fire and vowed never to write again.

She didn't mean it, of course. She couldn't stop herself from writing. Just around the time of that poem's fiery funeral, she read a poem in the *Godey's Lady's Book* called *The Fringed Gentian* and before she had read it twice, she knew it by heart.

"Then whisper, blossom, in thy sleep
How I may upward climb
The Alpine path, so hard, so steep
That leads to heights sublime.
How I may reach that far-off goal
Of true and honoured fame
And write upon its shining scroll
A woman's humble name."

She was electrified by the poem. She cut it out of the magazine and pasted it in the "portfolio" where she kept her homework and her letter writing. It became both a prayer and a watchword whenever she was discouraged, not only then, when she was a young teenager, but all her life. She gave it to Emily in *Emily of New Moon* and she called her collection of memories *The Alpine Path* because the poem meant so much to her.

While most of Maud's poems were more like *Evening Dreams* and *The Monarch of the Forest*, not all of them were.

She had a fine talent for silly verse. In school, in her early years, Maud and Cousin Alma Macneill, who had a pretty good talent for them, too, had verse-writing contests. One day, when they were supposedly studying fractions, they were making up verses about their teacher, until she noticed the slates being furtively passed back and forth. Luckily the teacher didn't read the verses (this was not Izzy Robinson). All the same, Maud and Alma rubbed them out at once and were much too scared to write any more—at least in school.

Grandfather and Izzy Robinson had such terrible battles that eventually the teacher moved out and Grandfather forbade Maud to go to school for as long as Miss Robinson was teaching there. This was in the early months of the year 1887 and it meant that, for the rest of Maud's twelfth year and half of her thirteenth, she had to keep up with her school work as best she could at home with the help of Amanda and Pensie—when she was allowed to get together with them. It was over a year later and she was almost fourteen before she was allowed to go back to school.

That year, she wrote a lot of poems and stories and long, loving letters to her father and to her new stepmother. Her father had never returned to Prince Edward Island after that one visit three years earlier. He had settled in the pioneer town of Prince Albert on the North Saskatchewan River in the Saskatchewan territory and now, this year, had married again. Maud only knew him, in these years, through the letters they exchanged. The letters she wrote were not saved but the loneliness and love for him she poured into them must have been a lot like the letters Jane wrote to her father in *Jane of Lantern Hill* and the bereaved Emily wrote to her dead father in *Emily of New Moon*.

During the months that she was kept out of school, Maud played alone on the shore in the huge hollow rock formation they all called the hole-in-the-wall, listening to the *sh-sh-sh* of the waves and the screeching of the gulls, making up stories about sailors drowning in dark, wild storms or mermaids riding the shining waves. She spent hours in the woods picking violets and out in the spring orchard "drinking in" the fragrance of the apple blossoms that surrounded her and watching the robins and goldfinches build their nests. Although she didn't really play with them anymore, she told stories to her dolls and, out in the barn, to her cats—like Sara Stanley in *The Story Girl,* Maud "would probably have known a story and tried to tell it if she were being led to the stake" no matter who was listening.

Grandmother arranged for her to take piano lessons from Mrs. Spurr, the Baptist minister's wife and to practice across the road on the parlour organ in Uncle Jimmy's house. (A few years later, her father and grandmother got together to buy her a parlour organ of her own.) She liked Mrs. Spurr ("plain but merry of face") and she liked the piano. Music and the playing of a musical instrument never became what words and writing were to Maud—she never had music-listening sprees as she had book sprees, even when she was many years older and had a radio. She liked it, though, and music remained a valuable companion throughout her life.

That summer of 1887 she went for a visit to Malpeque (about twenty kilometres southwest of Park Corner on Malpeque Bay) to see Aunt Emily and Uncle John Montgomery. Grandmother Montgomery died in Park Corner that summer and Maud went to the funeral. She had never been close to this grandmother but she mourned her loss and, perhaps even more, she hated that Grandfather Montgomery's home would be different now. Maud hated change at twelve just as much as she had done at seven, as she did, in fact, all her life.

When she came home that fall she helped dig potatoes and turnips and pick apples. She went to church on Sunday, to prayer meeting in the middle of the week (now that she was too old for Sunday School) and, once in a while, when her grandparents allowed her to go, she went to the new Literary Society meetings, where there were lectures and poetry recitations. Maud looked forward to those meetings with almost breathless anticipation. At no other time, in no other way, could she hear new ideas talked about or poetry read.

Izzy Robinson resigned from her post halfway through the next year. Hattie Gordon came to teach and Grandfather allowed Maud to go back to school. She was almost fourteen. With a feeling that life was once more as it should be, she slipped into her old place in the classroom beside Amanda. She wrote in her journal that Hattie Gordon was "a very different type of woman and teacher from Izzy Robinson. She was not faultless; but she was a lady, which Miss R. was not, and she had a certain stimulating personality . . . She had the power of inspiring love of study for its own sake and of making the dry bones of the school routine come alive with interest." Hattie Gordon was the model for Anne's beloved Miss Muriel Stacy in *Anne of Green Gables*.

A boy named Nathan Lockhart, the stepson of the Baptist minister (and son of Maud's piano teacher), had come to school and was "best chums" with Jack Laird. Nate was something of a tease and it wasn't long before he was calling Maud and Amanda, "Polly and Molly" because they were so close. Maud turned right around and called Nate and Jack, "Snip and Snap" and the names stuck for the rest of their school years.

Nate was a tall, skinny, curly-haired boy with freckles all over his pale face. He was fun and he was funny. Maud soon discovered that she would "have to work" to keep her top student place in school. A rivalry sprang up between them over the next couple of years which must have inspired the one Maud gave Anne Shirley and Gilbert Blythe, although hers and Nate's was friendlier. She also discovered, to her delight, that he devoured books as greedily as she did and the two of them exchanged their favourite books, then spent hours afterwards discussing every word in them. Together, they invented a "cipher" no one else could understand and, in that code, passed notes back and forth in school.

Over those next two-and-a-half years at the Cavendish school, Maud and Amanda, Nate and Jack and the others who had been sitting in that room together, almost all of them from grade one—Asher Robertson, Chesley Clark, Clemmie Macneill, Annie Stewart, Nellie Macneill, Alma Macneill, Maggie Clark, Lottie Simpson, Pensie's brother Russell—began to feel like "the old crowd." By the time they were fifteen in grade ten, some of the boys and girls were writing love letters to each other and scratching their names on the porch walls with hearts drawn around them.

Maud wasn't a bit interested in love letters or writing her name with any boy's and drawing a heart around it. She liked school. She liked helping to put on the concerts of singing and recitation that Miss Gordon was directing. She liked going on Miss Gordon's nature walks and sitting around with the old crowd having a "gabfest." But her head was full of poems and stories and she was intent on getting her education.

She didn't mind going along with the fun, though. There was a game they all played, a bit like the one when you pull petals from daisy heads to choose a future husband or wife. This game was played at night when the stars were out. You had to count nine stars for nine nights in a row and then the first boy you shook hands with, if you were a girl, would be the one you would marry, and the other way round if you were a boy. Maud and Amanda started counting their stars in November, just around the time of Maud's fifteenth birthday, but gave the game up when they still hadn't finished by the middle of February. Nate had counted his stars long since and Maud wheedled and wheedled him to tell her the name of the girl he had shaken hands with. "His Fair Unknown," she called the mystery girl. Finally, to get him to tell her, she had to promise to divulge a secret she knew, plus the name of the boy whose hand she would first shake when she got her stars "counted out."

When Nate passed her a note in school telling her that she was the one he had first shaken hands with, she didn't know what to do, how to respond. "Of course I like Nate best," she wrote in her journal that night, "He is very nice and we have always been chummy. But owning up to it in plain English is quite another thing. Besides, he may think the admission means a great deal more than it really does."

She wrote him a note saying that she liked him, too, because he had "a little more brains than the other Cavendish boys" and that she liked brains. The next morning he passed her another note (written in red ink) that said not only did he like her best but that he loved her.

Now she *was* shaken! She stood by herself "down in the school woods that winter morning under a big grey maple blushing over that note . . ." She had to admit to herself that she had "a queer, foolish triumphant little feeling about it" but she feared Nate's confession was going to spoil their friendship. She was at an age when some in her class, both boys and girls, were already thinking of marriage and she was a very attractive girl, slight and slim and vivacious. Her hair had darkened to a rich brown and she wore it in a single braid down her back. Her thin, little face had rounded to a soft oval. Her clear grey eyes held a hint of mischief in them, her small mouth often had a humourous quirk at the corners and her wit was quick and sharp. More than one boy was eager to walk her home from school and church and Literary Society meetings.

She found having a boy wanting to be her boyfriend more exciting than she'd had any idea it could be. And, if she was to have one, of course she'd rather have Nate than anyone. So she tried with all her might to care for him "in that way." But she couldn't. They wrote each other letters every night about their dreams and ambitions and they lingered for hours "under star-lit summer skies . . . around garden gates and . . . talk—talk—talk." But she didn't like kissing him. She wrote a few "mushy" letters in answer to his "mushy" ones and then was afraid he'd take them seriously. For a while he did. He wanted to talk about how they would marry one day. She didn't like him saying that. She just could not be serious about the whole business. The sad truth was that part of what she liked best about it was that she was "getting square" with Clemmie Macneill for a lot of slights and insults. Clemmie was "gone on Nate."

The school year was coming to an end. All the school years were coming to an end and the comradeship of the years together was much more important to Maud than worrying about hostilities or crushes. She stopped writing about those in her journal. Most of what she wrote about during the last days of school was the joy and the fun of that comradeship.

On a Saturday late in May, a few of the old crowd decided to clean the school because it hadn't been cleaned all year and it didn't look as though the school trustees were going to get around to it. What a day they had! Nate, Jack, Clemmie, Nellie, Chesley, Maggie and Maud set to with a will. It was pouring rain that day so they couldn't set their water bucket over an outside fire. They had to set it inside on the stove. Whistling and singing and making jokes, they took down all the blinds and maps and, when the water was hot, scrubbed a year's dirt from them. They washed the blackboard, then took the chalk erasers to the porch door and beat them together until the air was clear of chalk dust. They cleaned all the desks, the windows, the doors, the wainscotting and, finally, the floor. It was a job for Hercules, they all agreed, but they got it done and everything was as clean and neat as Grandmother's kitchen until Jack went to put out the fire in the stove with a bucketful of water.

He opened the door of the stove and hurled the whole bucketful into the roaring fire. "And, oh, such a cloud of boiling water, ashes, steam and soot burst out in Jack's face," wrote Maud in her journal that night, "He gave an unearthly whoop and fell over backward, spilling what water was left in the bucket all over himself, while the awful smell of the gas was what somebody has called 'deafening.' I thought Jack was killed but when he picked himself up with a real live 'cuss word,' I concluded he wasn't. But his face was all splattered with soot and he did look so funny."

Most of the day's hard work had to be done all over again but, when Maud was writing about it that night, it was the ridiculousness of Jack's accident she wrote about, ending with, "I shall never forget the look of Jack!"

In the final school concert in June, Jack gave the opening speech (and did not talk about dousing the fire in the stove), Maud played *The Swedish Wedding March* on the piano, and the whole school recited *The Ship on Fire*. School was over. "I fear we will never all be togther again," wrote Maud, "But no matter where we roam, a tie of common friendship will always bind us in memory."

CHAPTER 6

Prince Albert, Saskatchewan

"If one could but fly in the darkness over rivers and mountains and forests to the Island . . .—JANE OF LANTERN HILL

On Thursday, April 22, 1890 Maud wrote in her journal, "I may take a trip out west to see father this summer. . . . I feel so excited about it. It will be such a splendid trip. And then to see darling father again! I am frightened to think or say much about it for fear I will not get there after all."

She did get there. She was fifteen years old that year and Grandfather Montgomery was making a trip to Vancouver in August with a stopover in Saskatchewan to visit Maud's father, and stepmother and their baby daughter, Katie. Maud was to travel with him. The plan was that she would stay with her father and stepmother and two-year-old Katie in Prince Albert and go to high school there.

The night before she left home, she wrote, "I feel excited about starting away tomorrow—and a little blue, too. I've never travelled any but I think I'll like that; but what about Prince Albert? Shall I like it? And my stepmother? I do not know. She seems nice from her letters and I mean to love her if I can, just as if she were really my mother."

Goodbyes had been said to all her friends and, the next day, with a last tearful good-bye to her grandmother and grandfather, a last hug for each of the cats, Maud left Cavendish with her uncle Charles Crosby, who came from Park Corner to drive her to Grandfather Montgomery's. The sky was grey but the day was warm and the two chatted easily as the buggy bumped along the dusty road, but Maud's mind was not really on the conversation, her uncle, or even the meadows and woods along the way. Her mind was in a turmoil of thoughts and questions. It wasn't just because of the trip west. Grandfather had arranged for them to travel to Summerside on the special train that was carrying Prime Minister John A. Macdonald and his wife on a tour through the Island—the prime minister was a good friend of Senator Montgomery's. Would she be dressed properly to meet the prime minister? What could a fifteen-year old say to Lady Macdonald?

In Park Corner, Maud greeted her grandfather joyfully. She had a wonderful evening gossiping and giggling with Stella and Clara (George felt he was too old now to gossip with the girls and Frede was still a little girl), but it was soon over. It was raining when she got up in the morning but, all the same, dressed as she was in her good travelling suit and hat, Maud had to dash out to sniff the roses one more time and say one last farewell to her "Lake of Shining Waters." Then she hugged and kissed everyone and then did it again before she climbed into the buggy beside her grandfather.

They boarded the prime minister's special train in Kensington and, that night, in Summerside, Maud wrote that Sir John A. Macdonald was "very genial . . . a spry-looking old man—not handsome but pleasant-faced" and that "Lady M. is quite stately and imposing, with very beautiful silver hair, but not at all good looking and dressed . . . I thought, very dowdily (Maud had not grown out of her love of clothes and always noticed what people wore). That evening she and Grandfather attended a reception for the prime minister in splendid rooms where flowers and music and heavenly morsels to eat—and women in elegant evening gowns—presented more glamour than she had ever dreamed up for her childhood stories of lords and ladies in their castles.

The two Montgomerys left the next morning by steam ferry for Saint John, New Brunswick. From there they took the train to Montreal, where they spent a night and a day. Maud wrote, "I am sure I would not like to live here." Of course she would not; Maud never really wanted to live anywhere but on the Island, more particularly in Cavendish, and she was never truly happy away from there. All the same, she pronounced Montreal, "a fine city."

Then they were off across Ontario, where she did not think much of "the northern wilds" ("Rocks are all well enough in their way") except for Lake Superior, where she could imagine that she was "down on the shore at home." She thought the prairie was "the nearest approach to a desert" she had ever seen, with only, now and again, huge piles of buffalo bones for scenery. They arrived at the train station in Regina, at last, and there was her father to meet them. What a wonderful surprise! Maud wrote in her journal that night, "I laughed and cried. Oh it was so delightful to see dear father again. He hasn't changed at all, although it is five years since I saw him. Such a day this has been!"

It took two days to get to Prince Albert from Regina, first

as far as Duck Lake in "a strange little van" that ran on the railroad track, which Maud said was called a caboose. From there they rode in a wagon without springs called a buckboard and finally, to her relief, in a more comfortable buggy. She loved the prairie flowers, especially the bluebells, that became more and more abundant as they approached the North Saskatchewan River.

When they reached Prince Albert late in the afternoon, Maud met her stepmother and little Katie. That night she wrote in her journal that Prince Albert was "quite a pretty little town" but three days later, when Grandfather Montgomery left for the west coast, she wrote that she was "desperately homesick." When he stopped for a visit on his homeward journey in mid-September, she was almost sick, she wanted so badly to go home with him, but school had begun and she was enrolled for the year. She was resolute, she wanted her education.

A month later, when the Canadian Pacific Railway came to Prince Albert from Regina, Maud was there with the rest of the townspeople to watch Saskatchewan's lieutenant governor drive the last spike into the track. All that mattered to her about the arrival of train service in Prince Albert was that letters to and from Cavendish would travel faster.

She wrote letters to everyone—once a week, dutifully, to her Grandmother Macneill and to Frank and Prescott, regularly to her old teacher Hattie Gordon, to her Campbell and Crosby cousins in Park Corner, to several old classmates in Cavendish and to Nate Lockhart at college in Wolfville, Nova Scotia (whose letters to her had in them, " . . . a little sentimental nonsense . . . but not much"). She wrote most frequently to Pensie, Amanda and Lucy.

Maud's letters to Pensie, all of which Pensie saved and later stored away in the attic of her house, told about what was going on and what friends she was making in Prince Albert. In them she described the town and the countryside but, what she said over and over again was how she yearned to be home. "I cannot realize that I am over 3,000 miles away from the dear fields where we used to have such fun . . . I'm dreadfully lonely and homesick . . . oh, dear I do wish I was back on the dear old island . . . oh I couldn't live another year in this place if I were paid a thousand dollars an hour . . . it is dreadful to be among strangers all the time."

It wasn't just being among strangers or being away from her beloved Island. Maud liked Prince Albert. She wrote in her journal, "P.A. is built on several natural 'terraces' along the river bank, with 'bluffs,' as the hills are called, behind it sloping back to wide, rolling prairies dotted with groves of willow and poplar and countless tiny blue lakelets. Across the river are great pine forests and the views upstream are very beautiful." She wrote of the golden leaves on the aspen trees in autumn, the glories of tobogganing in winter and the beauty of the sudden prairie spring. Aside from the homesickness, most of what ruined Prince Albert for Maud was her stepmother.

Mary Ann McRae was born and raised in Cannington, Ontario. She moved to Saskatchewan when her widowed mother married a man who became a Dominion Land Agent in Prince Albert. She was twenty-four, round and pretty. She was used to comfort and was probably looking forward to a glittering social life with a politically promising husband when she married Hugh John Montgomery. He was, after all, the son of a Canadian senator. He was a forty-six-year-old widower whose only daughter lived thousands of miles away. He was handsome, full of energy and good humour and, though he did have his enemies, he was generally well liked everywhere he went.

Mary Ann and Hugh John Montgomery eventually had four children and, despite Hugh John's uneven career, they had a fairly comfortable life.

Maud wrote in her journal on August 23rd, "It is lovely to be with father again, he is such a darling. His eyes just shine with love when he looks at me. I never saw anyone look at me with such eyes before.

"But, to speak plainly I am afraid I am *not* going to like his wife. I came here prepared to love her warmly and look upon her as a real mother, but I fear it will prove quite impossible. I have been here only three days and already my eyes have been opened by several little things. For instance this morning at breakfast she did not pour any tea for me. Of course I knew this was just an oversight and waited for a minute or two after the others had begun eating before asking for it . . . but before I could speak she turned to me and said, in the most cutting and insulting tone of voice I ever heard and with the blackest look, 'What are you waiting for, Maud?' . . . I shall never forget that tone and the look that accompanied it! I answered quietly, 'my tea, please' and she looked silly enough, poured out the tea, slammed it down before me with such force that the tea spilled out of the cup in the saucer, and hardly spoke a word to anyone the rest of the meal.

"She also informed father yesterday that she wanted him to stop calling me 'Maudie' as it was entirely too childish. I believe it is the affection implied . . . of which she disapproves

. . . She seems to have a dreadful disposition—sulky, jealous, underhanded and *mean.*"

Mary Ann did not improve. On October 6, Maud wrote, "Mrs. Montgomery—I cannot call her anything else, except before others for father's sake—has, I think, the most dreadful disposition ever put into the heart of a woman."

Mary Ann was expecting her second child in the winter. Maud hoped that her stepmother's disposition would improve after the baby's birth, but she was sadly disappointed. Baby Bruce was born in February, but the only change in Maud's relationship to her stepmother was that she was now expected to walk the baby at night when he cried, in addition to her other household duties.

She was determined to put up with it for her father's sake but it wasn't easy and she often retreated to her room shaking with rage and humiliation. "There is no use in writing anything more about her," she wrote angrily one night, "Besides, I am constantly afraid she will sometime find and read this journal, although I keep it locked up. She reads all my letters and everything else she can find in my room when I am out."

She did not write about her dislike of her stepmother in the letters Pensie Macneill saved in her attic trunk but Maud, the keen-eyed, keen-eared, keen-minded girl with the amazing memory for both the actions and words of people, who had missed little that went on in her Cavendish neighbourhood, was as observant as ever. How much must Jane Stuart's Grandmother Kennedy in *Jane of Lantern Hill,* all those dreadful aunts of Valancy Stirling's in *The Blue Castle* and Emily Starr's Aunt Ruth, who makes life so hideous in *Emily Climbs,* owe to Mary Ann Montgomery and her disagreeable ways!

The year in Prince Albert wasn't all misery and unpleasant people. Maud loved her golden-haired little half-sister ("the dearest sweetest prettiest little angel you can imagine," she wrote to Pensie). She loved the family's scruffy little black cat, even though she thought he "wasn't a very nice fellow," and she wept when he died. She loved Bruce, the new baby, when he was born in February. And, although she feared that she would have no friends in this far—away place, it wasn't so. Despite her sharp tongue, with her quick wit and her high-spiritedness, Maud never had trouble finding friends. And, with her loving and loyal nature, she never had trouble keeping them. She had what Anne Shirley had, "a genius for friend-ship." She threw herself into the fun of fall hay rides out into the country, tobogganing and skating in winter, and baseball games in spring—Maud was a most enthusiastic baseball play-er. She taught Sunday school, she went to "Bible study," and she took part in school plays, the recitations or the tableaux that were so fashionable at the time.

A girl named Edith Skelton, the same age as Maud, was boarding with the Montgomerys when Maud arrived. They shared a bedroom and the two teenage girls, both far from home, were soon fast friends (Edith did not like Maud's step-mother, either). They started school together on the first of September and spent all their time together until Edith went home to Battleford a month later.

Maud missed Edith but she was so busy trying to get along at home and learning about life in this new community and her new school that she didn't have time to be lonely. She found her school books and the teacher's unfamiliar methods hard to get used to. And the school building was "bizarre." It was an old hotel. The high school was in one of its downstairs rooms and right above it was the ballroom where town functions often took place. When that happened, the high school room was used as a ladies' dressing room and the students always found things like hairpins, hand mirrors, dead flowers and feathers that had come off hats, strewn about the floor the next morning. And the room always smelled of face powder on those mornings. Rooms in the rest of the building were used for town council chambers, meetings of the Freemasons, and the Prince Albert town jail (complete with two Mounties permanently on guard).

"When they arrested a drunken man," Maud wrote Pensie, "they brought him in there, taking him through the hall outside our room, where very often there would be a lively scuffle and language strong enough to stand alone."

There were three girls and six boys in the high school class. John Mustard was a poor teacher with a violent temper who couldn't begin to keep order the way Hattie Gordon could keep it in all ten grades in the Cavendish school. He was a small, thin man, timid and nervous. He often beat the boys with a "murderous-looking 'raw-hide' whip as long as himself." The boys did not take to this readily. Some of them were as big as he was and, sometimes, one of them would grab a chunk of firewood and fight back. Then, wrote Maud, "the thing got quite sensational." There was more than this, however, to cause Maud to dislike her teacher.

One evening when her father was out and her stepmother was upstairs, Maud opened the door to a knock and there was Mr. Mustard, come to call. As he was from the same town in Ontario as her stepmother, this did not seem strange. It was certainly irritating, though, to find that, because Mary Ann had already gone to bed, she, herself, had to entertain the unwelcome guest all evening. He was "such a bore!" and he stayed and he stayed until she feared he "would never go."

He came again a few evenings later and then again and again. Every time he came there was some reason for her stepmother to be somewhere else, until Maud was forced to realize—although it took her a month or so—just what was going on. Mr. Mustard was courting her—and with her step-mother's "connivance."

Maud was outraged. She was sixteen that November, busy planning to further her education for a life that would allow her to write. She was not thinking of marriage. Moreover, she had not wanted any of "that sentimental non-sense" from her good friend Nate Lockhart and she certainly did not want it from her disagreeable, boring teacher, John Mustard, to whom she always referred in her journal as "Mustard"or "old Mustard."

Maud found a new friend in December. Laura Pritchard came into Prince Albert from the country for the winter to board with her aunt, who lived next door to the Montgomerys. She was going to go to the Roman Catholic convent school in town. She more than filled the gap Edith Skelton had left. When she and Maud had known each other for a few months, Maud wrote in her journal that she had never met a girl she could confide in as she could Laura. "We are twin spirits in every way." It may be, as close as Maud was to Pensie, Lucy and Amanda, that Laura Pritchard was her model for Diana Barry, Anne Shirley's kindred spirit in *Anne of Green Gables*. Maud never once called any of her

Cavendish friends, "twin spirits" and she dedicated *Anne's House of Dreams* to Laura.

The temperature outside was ranging from forty to sixty degrees below zero Fahrenheit. Mary Ann was becoming more demanding and John Mustard was beginning to really bother Maud—in school and out of it. The courtship was the subject of local gossip and even Maud's father had taken to making jokes about it. Maud begged Laura to come in the evenings and "torment Mustard terribly." She did. The two girls would sit in the parlour—nearest the stove—and make jokes at the teacher's expense. It did no good. Mustard was not to be deterred. He came almost every evening, no matter how cold, no matter how snowy. As well, he made life difficult for Maud in school, favouring her in class, gazing, cow-eyed, at her all the day long. The description of the moustache-curling Mr. Phillips "making eyes" at Prissy Andrews in *Anne of Green Gables* is taken directly from the eyes John Mustard made at Maud Montgomery in the Prince Albert high school.

What's more, he was jealous of her friends—particularly boy friends and Maud had many. There were boys who sent her presents she didn't want and offered to take her places she didn't want to go. She did like being popular, so she went out with some of them, but there was only one boy she really liked. He was Laura Pritchard's brother Will. Will came to Prince Albert in December with Laura to enter Maud's high school class and Maud liked him at once.

She described him in her journal—a "splendid" boy with red hair, green eyes and a crooked mouth. He was quiet and thoughtful, he liked to read and he had a keen sense of humour. He walked Maud home from school every afternoon and carried her books—and how jealous that made "old Mustard"! Will went to Sunday school and Bible study with Maud and Laura. In class he and Maud passed notes to each other in cipher (the same one that Maud and Nate Lockhart had devised a couple of years earlier back in Cavendish).

Then, in March, Maud had to quit school. Her stepmother had given up trying to keep hired girls to look after the children and the house. Not one would stay with her, she was so disagreeable. Instead, she kept Maud home to do the work so that she could pursue her social life. Maud's father, anxious to keep the peace, did not interfere. Maud must have hated it, but she wrote nothing about it in her journal except for the occasional bitter word. For the first time in her life, she was depressed for several days at a time.

She saw her friends at church, in Sunday school where she was teaching, and in Bible study. In his own quiet way, Will Pritchard continued to be as faithful a swain as Mustard—and as welcome as Mustard was not. In spite of the far-below-freezing temperatures and the biting winter winds, he went on walks along the frozen river with Maud, bought her little bags of "vanilla creams" and brightened her days with his jokes and cheerful talk.

Spring came in a sudden glory of crocuses, bluebells and the rush of water as the ice broke up in the river. Summer was not far behind. Maud's year in Prince Albert was drawing to a close. Will and Maud were on their way home from the Bible study picnic on the last day of July, riding in an open tram-car on a seat opposite Laura and her boyfriend. A sudden thunderstorm came up and the rain came down in torrents. Maud and Will snuggled under Will's umbrella and, in Maud's words, "had a nice little talk." A few days later they exchanged photographs, rings and ten-year letters. So did Maud and Laura. Ten-year letters were very popular at that time. Friends would write letters describing what they thought they would be doing in ten years, exchange the letters, and promise not to read them until the ten years had passed.

"Perhaps we'll be reading them together," said Will, shyly. It gave Maud a little thrill to hear him say that, but she didn't really think it would be so. She had the same kind of feeling for Will that she had for Nate Lockhart. "I *like* Will better than any boy I ever met but I *know* I don't love him—he just seems like a brother or a jolly good comrade to me," she wrote that night.

A week or so later, John Mustard got up the courage to propose marriage. He did it during one of his endless evenings in the Montgomerys' parlour. Maud was sitting in a corner of the sofa, holding her sleeping baby brother on her lap. Late sunlight filtered through the lace curtains at the window opposite. Mustard was sitting across the room in a rocking chair. For a long time he stared out the window, fidgeting with his hands, saying nothing. Maud "glared at a length of yellow yarn on the carpet." Finally, Mustard turned from the window, "with a very ghastly sort of smile" on his face.

"D-do you think, Miss Montgomery, that our friendship will ever develop into anything else?" he stammered.

"I don't see what else it can develop into, Mr. Mustard," answered Maud firmly. She had expected "to be flustered" but she wasn't, although she certainly wished herself "a thousand miles away."

"It's just as you think." he said slowly. Then he added fervently, with tears in his eyes, "I hope y-you weren't offended."

Maud assured him that she wasn't. After what seemed to her like centuries of time, Mustard got up, stuttered a good-bye and left. That night Maud wrote in her journal, "I am devoutly thankful that the dreaded ordeal is over." What she didn't say here—or anywhere in her journals, but says about Emily in *Emily Climbs*—may have been true of herself during the evening's event: "Under all her discomfort and dread, there was *Something* that was standing back and *enjoying* this—the drama, the comedy of it." There was about Maud that sense that there was "*Something*" in her that stood back and watched and enjoyed. It was the something that made her not only the person, but the writer that she was.

A few weeks later she left Prince Albert, but she left with more than the memory of John Mustard's proposal, her disagreeable stepmother, the love of Will Pritchard and the friendship of his sister Laura. She left with her first real writing triumph under her belt. In November she had written a poem based on an old Prince Edward Island legend about a spot where she and her friends had always played, *The Legend of Cape Leforce,* and had sent it to *The Charlottetown Patriot.* She had told no one. One day in early December, in the mail from the Island, there, with no forewarning, was the paper with her poem in it.

"I grew dizzy, the letters danced before my eyes and I felt a curious sensation of choking," she wrote that night. " . . . Father was so pleased and I am so glad and elated and happy. I can't find words to express my feelings." For Maud Montgomery this was rare indeed.

A few months later another poem was accepted by the *Patriot.* Then she was invited to write an article for the Saskatoon paper about her impressions of Saskatchewan. How she revelled in the "kudos" she got from her neighbours, her schoolmates and her friends.

Maud left Prince Albert early on the morning of August 27th. She was overjoyed to be going home. She was relieved to be leaving her stepmother, but she knew she would miss Katie and the baby, and saying goodbye to her father was agonizing. Having to say goodbye to Laura and Will was almost as bad. The sun was bright that morning and there was a whole crowd of friends at the station to see her off, so she steeled herself not to cry until the train pulled out of the station and "Laura's face passed out of sight." Then she had her cry, but by the time she had gone three miles she had dried her eyes. She was beginning to fully realize that the year was over. She was, at last, "homeward bound."

CHAPTER 7

Home Again

"And then . . . it came on you so suddenly and beautifully as you stepped over the crest of the hill field. It welcomed you like a friend with all its windows astir."—PAT OF SILVER BUSH

Maud sprang down from the train at the stone station in Kensington on a warm September evening. She looked eagerly all around her, then flew across the road to the hotel, where she hired a driver with a horse and buggy to take her to Park Corner. In no time at all, she had her luggage stashed and was on her way. The thought, 'I'm home, I'm home' kept singing in her head, as it had been doing ever since the moment she'd smelled the tang of the sea. She'd hardly been able to contain herself when she finally caught sight of the "distant green hills" of her island from the boat crossing the Northumberland Strait.

It had taken ten days by train and boat to get to Prince Edward Island from Prince Albert, Saskatchewan. Now, at last, here she sat, her hat in her lap, her long, dark hair waving in the cool sea breeze as she jounced along the road behind the horse, chattering excitedly to the driver.

"How I did enjoy that drive!" she wrote that night in her

journal, "It was all so lovely—the beautiful sunset, the rich harvest scenery, and the aroma of the firs along the road. I just gazed my eyes out. And when we came in sight of the sea I could not speak for emotion. I listened to its hollow roar in unspeakable delight."

When she pushed open her grandfather's door in Park Corner, for a moment or two no one recognized the tall, grown-up-looking girl who stood before them. Nor did they at Aunt Annie's and Uncle John's across the road. But when they realized it was Maud, home from the west, what hugs and kisses and glad cries there were!

Three days later she was back in Cavendish. "I am at home—actually at home in dear old C." she wrote that night. There was never a place for Maud, no matter where she went or how old she got, that could equal home. To be home on the Island was a like a return to the garden of Eden, to be at home in Cavendish was to be in heaven itself.

She hugged everyone, "ran through every room in the house," rushed outside to greet the chickens and turkeys and hug Topsy (the cat who had replaced poor Pussy-willow), then set out around the entire village to greet her aunts, uncles, cousins, friends, her old teacher, Miss Gordon (who disappointed her by not being at home), the school, the church and every neighbourhood dog and cat she met along the way. She was home with her own Lover's Lane, her own Haunted Wood, her own Cavendish shore and sea, her own people.

Joyously she got down on her knees and buried her face in the sweet william and the pansies. She walked along the shore and through the woods and meadows, revelling in the salt-and-fish smell of the sea, the goldenrod and the purple farewell-summers along the roads and paths. She spent afternoons with Lucy, Amanda and Pensie "in the drowsy September sunshine" picking apples, "dodging Laird's cows," and reminiscing about school days. It was wonderful but, in spite of the pleasure she felt, she felt a little lost, in a way not quite as at home as she'd been before she went away. She wrote wistfully in her journal one night that it was, "as if we somehow belonged to those past days and had no business in the present at all." And her future seemed uncertain.

She knew that she could not hope to earn a living as a writer for many years, if ever. She would have to have some other source of income and there were not many ways for a woman to earn a living in 1891. She had decided, even before leaving for Saskatchewan, that her way was going to be teaching. So, as soon as she had properly settled in at home, Maud told her grandparents she wanted to go to Prince of Wales College in Charlottetown to study for a teacher's license. But, ever since the winter Izzy Robinson had boarded with him, Grandfather Macneill had turned against women teachers. Being the stubborn old man he was, he refused to pay a single penny towards an education that would get Maud her license.

Pleading with her grandfather did no good. She bit back angry words and hid her tears of frustration. She knew all too well, where they would lead. But Maud Montgomery was every bit as stubborn as her grandfather. She had never backed down from a challenge—or from going after what she really wanted. She didn't know how she was going to manage it, but she was determined she was going to get that teacher's license. So she set herself a course of study in the subjects she would need and she made herself sit down to work at it every day.

And, of course, she went right on plugging away at her writing. Her grandfather did not object to that. At his request, she wrote a "sketch" of her trip home from Prince Albert and sent it to *The Charlottetown Patriot,* the newspaper that had printed her story and poem the winter before when she had been out west. The editor of the paper was happy to print her sketch.

The *Patriot* also printed some of her poems, but her stories were coming back from newspapers and magazines as regularly as she was sending them out, in the same way Emily Starr's stories came back to her, "with only a little *printed slip* saying, 'We regret we cannot use this contribution.'"

Those rejections were terribly painful but nothing could permanently squelch a girl with Maud's perseverance—or her appetite for writing stories. "I wonder if I shall ever be able to do anything with my pen," she wrote disconsolately in her journal, "If I could only manage to get a little more education! . . . I wish I could peep into my future for a moment . . ."

But she couldn't. So she wrote and read—and dreamed. As they had always been for Maud, writing and reading and dreaming were often the same. That fall she was enthralled by a book called *Zanoni,* an occult love story written by an English nobleman named Edward Bulwer-Lytton. She read and re-read *Zanoni*—as she had once read and reread *Little Katey and Jolly Jim* and *The Memoir of Anzonetta Peters*—until she knew whole chunks of it by heart. She lived in the story as only a person with her intense nature, fertile imagination and love for the supernatural could do. She was so in love with its dark, masterful hero that she actually spent hours rewriting some of Lord Lytton's story so that the heroine's dialogue and behaviour would read more like dialogue and behaviour that would be hers if she were *Zanoni's* heroine.

Zanoni wasn't the only book she was reading. Along with her old school books, she read whatever she could find both for pleasure and to learn from their authors how to improve her own writing: religious tracts, newspapers, the *Godey's Lady's Book,* Charles Dickens's *Pickwick Papers,* Sir Walter Scott's novels, Nathaniel Hawthorne's, *The House of the Seven Gables,* Washington Irving's *The Sketch Book,* and Ralph Waldo Emerson's essays. She enjoyed them all but she did not live in any of them the way she lived in *Zanoni.*

That fall, Hattie Gordon was putting together a school concert and asked Maud and whoever else among her old pupils were in Cavendish to take part. Maud loved helping get concerts together and also reciting in them. She set to with a will to learn verses, make costumes, decorate the school and be on hand for the festive evening. The pleasure she found in that effort—and the success she made of it—became Anne Shirley's pleasure and her success in her recitations in *Anne of Green Gables.*

Then, in February, Aunt Annie Campbell invited her to Park Corner to give Stella, Clara, George and Frede piano lessons. Gratefully, Maud left her household chores and her studies behind and went. She'd never taught the piano, but this was like being given a holiday. The Campbell house always had fires in all its stoves. And it had kind Aunt Annie and Uncle John and the young people.

In Grandfather Montgomery's house across the way there were aunts, uncles and cousins coming and going but they would be coming and going very carefully and very quietly this winter, because Grandfather was very ill. Maud knew she wouldn't be able to spend more than a few moments at a time with him because he was too weak for a real visit and he had become almost totally deaf. She felt terribly sad about it because she had always loved her Grandfather Montgomery and she had grown close to him on their trip west together. She hoped her aunts would let her help nurse him so she could have a few moments with him once in a while.

But she was only seventeen years old and she had hungered for the jollity in the Campbells' household. Diligently she taught her three oldest cousins everything she'd learned in her own piano lessons, but there was still plenty of time for "larks." One afternoon, after the young people got home from school, they all made great piles of pancakes together on the big kitchen stove. They smothered them in maple syrup and butter and ate every one. That night, upstairs in the big feather bed they were sharing, Maud and Clara nestled under their heavy quilt and talked and laughed "until the pancakes nearly choked" them. On other nights, while the snow blew down the chimney and the wind rattled the windows, they all sat around the sitting-room stove and told ghost stories. Sometimes they skated on the pond and sometimes, because she so needed time to herself, Maud would go off into the woods alone. Then she would write in her journal words like Emily's in *Emily Climbs,* "I had a lovely time with myself this evening . . . The sun was low and creamy and the snow so white and the shadows so slender and blue."

One bright, moonlit night shortly after Maud arrived in Park Corner, all the young people crammed themselves into the cutter and, with sleigh bells jingling, went skimming along the icy roads to the Literary Society meeting in French River to hear a special lecture. They were hatted and gloved, well bundled up, and they enjoyed themselves, but it was very cold and the damp sea wind seemed to find its way even through the fur robes. They were glad to reach the warmth of the hall. For Maud it turned out to be an evening to remember. A man named Captain George McLeod complimented Maud on the story and poems that had appeared in the Charlottetown paper and told her to "keep on." (Her entry in that night's journal said, "Ta-ta, Capt. George, that is just what I mean to do.")

Then, to add to her feeling that she was surely the most important young woman in Prince Edward Island that night, not one, but two attractive young men took special notice of her. Lemuel McLeod, a Park Corner neighbour of the Campbells, came to speak to her during the evening-program's "social intermission." Then Edwin Simpson, a second cousin she'd never met, came to introduce himself. Maud had little to say about Lem in her journal that night, except that she'd had "a nice little chat" with him, but she wrote that Ed was good looking and had "fine eyes." A few weeks later Ed, who was at school in French River, walked home with her from "Literary" in Park Corner. She couldn't decide whether or not she liked him. She thought he was clever and could "talk about everything," but that he was *awfully* conceited—and worse, still, *Simpsony.*" (Simpsons were Maud's least favourite of the clan's families and not all that popular with other people.)

There were always boys to walk the girls home along the frozen roads after prayer or Literary Society meetings. Maud had found, during her year in Prince Albert, that she liked to flirt and there was always a boy eager to start up the spark in her eyes and duel with her bantering wit. Clara and Stella had their "beaux" too and the girls spent hours sighing and talking about them late into the night, cosied under their heavy quilts.

Chief among those young men happy to flirt with Maud were Lem McLeod and Ed Simpson. They became intense rivals for her company. At first she found it flattering, but after a time she grew tired of their persistence—and everyone else's teasing. Once at a Literary Society meeting Maud spent half the evening trying to figure out a way to escape them both.

"I made up my mind to rush right out the moment Literary adjourned and get away up the road before the boys could get out," she wrote in her journal. "I made a dive for the door— but so did everyone else apparently and I found myself packed in a crowded, squirming mass below the stove. I pushed frantically on, flattering myself that I was far ahead of the boys, when I discovered Lem right behind me and Ed right beside me. I was as mad as a wasp. I made a wild effort to get through the crowd and as a result got jammed in between the two of them! But at last we got to that blessed door. I clutched Clara's arm, bolted headlong down the steps, and gained the road in safety. But I hadn't got my breath before Lem had caught up with us; he gasped out a request to see me home and whisked me off before I could answer yea or nay. Since it had to be one of them I was glad it was Lem. Ed is much cleverer but somehow I never feel at ease in his company."

June came and with it an end to the Ed-and-Lem rivalry. Maud went home to Cavendish, her studies and her quieter home life. She missed her Park Corner relatives and the liveliness there, but she was glad to see her friends and she fell easily into her old routine of Literary Society and prayer meetings, Sunday church services, and long rambles in the soft summer evenings she called "twilight rackets" with her friends. Nate Lockhart and Jack Laird had both come home that summer from college, but Nate had already gone off for his summer job. Maud was sorry to have missed Nate but happy to see Jack.

Then one night Jack walked her home from Amanda's house after one of their "rackets." The moon was full, there was a gentle breeze and he began to talk "that sentimental nonsense" Maud hated. She turned his words aside with a joke. He persisted. She laughed and made fun of him. He told her he was serious, that he loved her. She laughed so hard that he turned away from her and wouldn't talk. They walked in silence for ten long minutes.

"When he saw that *that* didn't worry me any he got friendly and sensible again," Maud wrote in her journal that night, "Jack doesn't 'love' me any more than I love him. It was the moonlight." She was probably right, as he went right on being "friendly and sensible" and made her no further declarations of love.

She was relieved. Although she was eighteen, an age when many of her old classmates were getting married, she still wanted nothing to do with marriage. She was bent on becoming a writer and she wanted to go to college. She loved the shared talk and laughter of those evenings with her friends and she did enjoy casual flirtations but she thought, as Anne Shirley thought, that "boys were . . . good comrades." She did not want to play at love as she had done with Nate Lockhart in their last year at school or encourage that kind of attention from Jack Laird or put herself, however unwittingly, into a position where she could be courted by another John Mustard.

Dave and Well Nelson arrived for an unexpected visit. Like three old people, they and Maud reminisced about the great times they'd had as children, making play houses, story telling and reading together—and laughed about the *Wide Awake* serial Maud hadn't been able to finish. After the Nelsons left, Maud settled down again to her routine of work, walks and writing—stories, poems, daily journal entries and letters. She wrote to Laura and Will Pritchard in Prince Albert and, with much less pleasure, because in a weak moment she had promised, to John Mustard. What she was doing, without realizing it, was recording her life for the books she would one day write. Anne Shirley, engrossed in *The Lady of Shalott* and writing her melodramatic stories with their "high falutin language," Emily Starr at home in the days before college, Pat Gardiner contending with the changes at Silver Birch, all reflect those uneasy months Maud spent between coming home from Prince Albert and going off to college.

Because, wonder of wonders, unbeknownst to her, Grandmother Macneill and Maud's father had been corresponding about the problem of her education. They had agreed to share the cost of sending her to Prince of Wales College the following year. Grandfather Macneill would have nothing to do with it.

Maud could hardly believe her good fortune. Feeling like a cat contemplating a bowl of cream, she polished her boots, gathered up her books and went back to the little Cavendish school in order to have the teacher's help in preparing for the next July's entrance exams to the college.

Hattie Gordon had left in the spring to teach in the western United States. Maud felt she had lost not only a good teacher but "a true friend—the only one in Cavendish who sym-pathized with me in my ambitions and efforts." But she settled down in her old seat by the window where she could look "away down into the old spruce woods, with their shadows and sunlight and whispering." She enjoyed the companionship of the younger brothers and sisters of "the old crowd" but she did miss her friends. Although she didn't find the new teacher very help-ful, she studied hard all through the winter and spring and, almost too soon, it was July and she was off to Charlottetown in a state of terror to "put her fate to the test."

Her determination to go to college, her family pride and her need not to let her father and grandmother down all cried out to her, *You must succeed!* For three days she wrote exams in geography, agriculture, French, English, arithmetic, Latin, geometry and algebra. Twelve days later when "the pass list" was published in the Charlottetown newspapers, she found herself to be fifth out of two-hundred-and sixty-four candi-dates. As Anne Shirley said when she tied with Gilbert Blythe for first place in her exams to enter Queen's College, "that moment was worth waiting for."

In August Grandfather Montgomery died in Park Corner. It did not come as a great shock to Maud because he had been so ill, but she had truly loved this gruff, kind grandfather and she felt his loss sorely. Grandfather Macneill drove her to Park Corner in the buggy for the funeral. The beauty of the fields and brooks along the way might have been of some comfort to her, but Grandfather was not pleasant company. Then there were so many grieving relatives at the old house where Grandfather Montgomery would never be again that the whole day was dark and doleful.

But Maud had never been one to wallow in grief. She did what she always did in times of stress or sadness: she walked where she loved best to walk and, as Pat Gardiner did after her friend Betts died in *Pat of Silver Bush,* she "drew comfort and strength from its old, patient familiar acres." And then she tucked her grief away, as she had always done, and got on with her life.

CHAPTER 8

Charlottetown

"Oh, Marilla, thank you . . . I'll study as hard as I can and do my very best to be a credit to you. I warn you not to expect too much in geometry, but I think I can hold my own in anything else if I work hard."
—ANNE OF GREEN GABLES

September fifth, 1893 found Maud registering at Prince of Wales College in Charlottetown. She was going to do two years work in one for a first class certificate—she had decided she must do this for her father and grandmother and she was prepared to work hard. But she meant to have fun, too. She was almost nineteen years old. She was now wearing her dark hair pinned up in back with a soft, curled bang across her high forehead. There was purpose in her grey eyes, but there was still that sparkle, and there was that hint of humour lurking at the corners of her mouth. There was strength and determination in her step and she was more than ready to face this new challenge.

Charlottetown was the Island's capital and, as it was only about fifty kilometres southeast of Cavendish, Maud had been there quite a few times with her grandparents and to visit her

Sutherland and McIntyre relatives (Aunt Maggie Sutherland and Aunt Mary McIntyre were two of her father's sisters)—and, of course, to write her exams in the spring. It was a busy port city, with ships coming and going all the time but small enough not to completely overwhelm a girl from a little up-island village. Its market on the waterfront was a handsome wooden structure where you could see all manner of fish and farm produce and baking. Province House, facing the tall fountain in Queen Square Gardens, was truly splendid and the many church steeples that rose high over the rooftops were beautiful. And now there were electric lights along many of the paved streets. Along some of those streets were grand clapboard houses with towers and big verandahs, surrounded by deep lawns. Along other streets the houses were smaller, closer together, and not nearly as fine.

Prince of Wales College was only a short walk from the city centre. It was a large, square, two-storey building. It wasn't beautiful, but it had big, old hardwood trees here and there on its campus to soften its austere face. It housed the college classrooms and the teachers' offices. Student teachers took some of their classes there and some in the nearby Normal School, the teachers' training school.

At first Maud was afraid she would never get used to it and never get along with her classmates. Like Anne Shirley at Queen's College, she felt "such a pang of loneliness when she found herself in a room with fifty other students, not one of whom she knew . . ." She wrote in her journal that they seemed an "unacquaintable lot." And Mrs. MacMillan's boardinghouse, recommended to her grandmother, was on a little side street and it was dark and dingy. She did like her roommate, Mary Campbell (a distant cousin). Mary was a small, pretty, dark-haired girl, even-tempered and fun to be with. Maud realized that Mary was "a little afraid" of her, and of her "sarcastic tongue and unfailing and unsparing raillery," but Mary had such a sunny nature and Maud liked her so much that the two of them had a good year together in "Mrs. Mac's" big upstairs room.

It didn't take Maud very long after all to get used to the school. Only five days after her first class, she was writing in her journal "I love going to college. It is simply delightful . . . I am not homesick—I have never been a bit homesick since I came to town . . ."

The days were warm and soft. The leaves on the hardwood trees hadn't yet begun to change colour and the marigolds and chrysanthemum were still in bloom in all the gardens. Between and after classes and at dinner time the students sat around on the grass under the shade trees and got to know each other. As she always did, Maud made friends. She went boating; she went on outings out into the country and to church, and to evening lectures, concerts and plays at the Opera House. As always, too, she was much sought after by boys wanting to walk her home from all the evening events.

Among them was her old Park Corner admirer, Lem McLeod. He had come to Charlottetown to go to Business College and he and Maud met by chance one afternoon when they were both out walking. He came the very next evening to call on her. Maud thought Lem was "a nice jolly lad," but that, if she saw him once a week for "a newsy chat" it was "quite enough." It wasn't quite enough for Lem and he came often. Maud did not want him to pursue her as ardently as he had done back in Park Corner, but she liked him too much to tell him not to call.

There were other boys whose interest in Maud was as comradely as hers was in them. Three of them lived in Mrs. MacMillan's boardinghouse. One was Mary Campbell's brother Norman, who arrived in the early fall. The other two came partway through the fall term: Stewart, one of Maud's Simpson cousins (but not too "Simpsony") and his friend Jim Stevenson. Jim was as voracious a reader as Maud. He also liked to write and was every bit as competitive as she was. They were soon engaged in the same kind of rivalry she'd had with Nate Lockhart back in the old Cavendish schoolhouse. Evenings at "Mrs. Mac's" were never boring.

Maud did like one boy in a little more than the "comradely" way she liked most boys. He was her cousin Jack Sutherland. Maud had always liked her Sutherland relatives, although until now she had never seen much of them. She didn't imagine herself to be deeply in love with Jack but she did take "a violent fancy" to him. She described him in her journal as being "six feet of young manhood . . . a tall, homely fellow but with something very charming in his personality." There was always a little extra sparkle in her eye when he came to call. And it was always a thrill to run into him on the street or at social functions and to find him home when she went to call on Aunt Maggie—which she managed to do fairly often.

Maud threw herself into her schoolwork with all her usual all-or-nothing zest and, at the end of her second month of classes, she had her first practice-teaching session. She was very nervous about it. "Quakingly" she followed her professor into the schoolroom full of children at "the Normal." And, "quakingly," she "advanced to the front, announced the subject and plunged headlong in." Then, as she wrote that night in her journal, she "warmed up, forgot to be nervous and got on swimmingly." She was quite pleased with herself. And she got good marks.

But what made that fall sing for Maud was what she found one day when she got home from classes, only a few weeks after they had begun in September. There was a letter waiting for her with the name *The Ladies World Magazine* in flowery script and a return address in New York on its envelope. The editor had accepted a poem she'd sent them, titled *The Violet's Spell*, and was offering her two subscriptions to the magazine in payment—her first payment of any kind for a piece of writing. She wrote triumphantly in her journal that night, "It is a start and I mean to keep on." She did keep on, all through her college year, not only with the stories and poems she sent out to newspapers and magazines (and got right back again) but in *The College Record,* the school paper some of the boys had started.

Fall turned into winter. Mrs. MacMillan's was not only dark and dingy and the meals so badly cooked and so often exactly the same that Maud and Mary took to calling dinner "ditto." It was so cold that one winter morning the ice was two inches thick on the water jug in the bedroom. " 'Oh, mi dere diry,' as saith the famous 'Bad Boy,' this is awful! . . . I never saw such a cold house," Maud wrote in her journal. "The wind seems to blow through it like paper; besides Mrs. M. is very VERY V-E-R-Y economical in regard to coal. We are *never* warm except when we are in bed and not always then unless we pile every stitch of clothes we own on the bed and sometimes even the mats from the floor!" She was glad to be going home for Christmas.

The holiday came and went. Winter gradually turned into spring. In March, Lem McLeod's course was finished and he came to say goodbye to Maud. He told her how much he did not want to go away from her and hoped that he would see her very soon again. Determined to keep him from saying anything too "sentimental," she talked and laughed and made jokes frantically. She wrote in her journal that she was "frosty in the extreme" when it came time to say goodbye because she wanted so badly to keep at bay the "shade of seriousness" that their relationship had taken on. She never liked to say goodbye to friends, but Lem's departure was a worry lifted from her mind.

By this time Maud no longer felt at all "unacquainted" with her classmates. They had become a family of teachers-in-training, set on becoming responsible mentors of the young, but still at times kids "getting up larks." Maud was often one of the ringleaders when they played jokes on their professors. One afternoon in early March, during chemistry class—where they all disliked the professor, who was, "no good whatever as a teacher"—they had a "peanut party." It had been in the planning for days. Everyone in the class "had subscribed two cents" and two of the girls who had a free hour in the morning "sneaked off uptown and got four pounds of peanuts." The peanuts were quickly passed around and eaten. And then, "The air was thick with flying shells and beans, while a big carrot and a red herring also passed and repassed." Not much work was done in chemistry class that day.

A few weeks later, in another class, not because they disliked the professor but just out of high spirits because it was spring, all the girls crept into the room before class and mixed up everyone's books so thoroughly that it took at least half an hour to straighten them all out while their enraged professor shouted until he was "black in the face."

Only a couple of months later, there were no more classes to "get up larks" in. With May came two sets of final exams, one for graduation from college and one for the teaching license. There was much groaning, nail biting and late-night studying at Mrs. MacMillan's boardinghouse, but they all managed to get through their exams and Maud found only algebra to be a real "beast."

At the school year's end, Jim Stevenson earned the college medal and he was the class valedictorian, but Maud's rivalry with him, like Anne's with Gilbert in *Anne of Green Gables,* ended in a kind of tie because Maud was chosen to write an essay to read at the Commencement exercises. She chose to write about the character of Portia from Shakespeare's *The Merchant of Venice,* a play she had studied in her English course. In the end she wrote the valedictory speech, too, because Jim cajoled her until she gave in and wrote it for him.

On the evening of June eighth Maud stood on the stage of the Opera House with all her classmates before an audience made up of all their devoted friends and relatives. With her hair pinned up, dressed in her favourite cream-coloured challis dress with the ruffle at the neck and a bunch of fresh pansies at her waist, she looked cool and self-possessed. She wasn't. When she described Anne Shirley's "overwhelming attack of stage fright" at her recitation at the White Sands Hotel in *Anne of Green*

Gables, she had to be remembering that night. She was trembling. Her hands were icy. Her mouth was dry. But she read her essay on the character of Portia in a strong, clear voice. The applause was wonderful. But that wasn't all. The next day's *Charlottetown Guardian* had in it a paragraph praising the essay and that afternoon the editor himself, called to ask for a copy of the essay to print. The *Charlottetown Patriot* printed it, as well.

The year was over. Maud wrote in her journal, "I am F-R-E-E!" But the excitement of that ebbed almost as soon as she'd written the words. There were the sad farewells to say to her teachers and her classmates, to her McIntyre and Sutherland relatives (especially Cousin Jack), to Mary and Norman Campbell, to Stewart Simpson and Jim Stevenson. "Thus it goes," she wrote. "Just as soon as I meet and learn to love a friend we must part and go our separate ways, never to meet on quite the same ground again."

But, with Maud as with Anne Shirley at the end of her year at Queen's College, "All the Beyond was hers with its possibilities lurking rosily in the oncoming years—each year a rose of promise to be woven into an immortal chaplet."

THE VIOLET'S SPELL (first four verses)

Only a violet in the trodden street
Breathing its purple life out 'neath the tread
Of hundreds, restless, eager, hurrying feet,
Ere set of sun the frail thing will be dead;
"Only a violet," its loser said.

As in a dream the dusty street passed them
Unheeded on my ear its tumult fell;
I saw a vision from the past again
That wove across my heart a nameless spell—
Fond memories of a spot I once loved well.

A woodland lane where ferns grew green and tall,
And beeches wove their branches overhead,
All silence save some wild bird's passing call
Or the swift echoing of a rabbit's tread;
'Neath those green arches fear and strife were dead!

Blue smiled the sky where thro' the fir trees green
The summer sunshine fell in golden sheaves,
And shyly from beneath the mossy screen
With half-averted face as one who grieves,
Blue violets peeped thro' last year's withered leaves.

CHAPTER 9

Maud Montgomery, Teacher

"While the children read their verses Anne marshalled her shaky wits into order and looked over the little army of pilgrims to the Grown-up Land."
—ANNE OF AVONLEA

Maud went home to Cavendish well satisfied with herself and her year's work. Her plan was working. She really *was* going to work as a teacher while she perfected her writing and, maybe, someday would earn her living at it. But first, how was she to get a school? All the other hopeful teachers were driving to the villages where there were jobs in order to have personal interviews with school trustees. Maud couldn't do that. Grandfather Macneill refused to either drive her to interviews or to let her have a horse and buggy to drive herself. She had to rely on letters and they weren't bringing her any good results. Most of them weren't even answered. She was in despair until, finally, on the 26th of July, four days before the next school term was to begin, she was offered a job in Bideford on Malpeque Bay, about a hundred kilometres west of Cavendish.

"I don't know how I will succeed," she wrote the night

before she left, "but if hard and persevering work can bring me good fortune I am resolved that I can attain it."

Two days later, with her clothes, her books, her paper and her pens packed and ready, she left home once more. Lucy and Pensie arrived at five o'clock in the morning to drive her to the train station in Hunter River in Pensie's buggy. The skies were grey and "it was blowing a hurricane," but they had "a jolly drive" and got to the station in good time, the train came in and Maud was off.

In two days she was standing in front of a schoolroom full of children. There was the old familiar combination of the odours of years of chalk and wood-stove fires. There were the rows of benches and desks and there were twenty children between the ages of six and thirteen, all staring up at her, expecting her to be in charge. She took a deep breath, and feeling "forty different ways at once," put on her best schoolmarmish voice and started in. By four o'clock in the afternoon, she was so tired she wanted to "sit down and cry." And no teacher can ever have been more relieved than Maud was to see the end of his-or-her first week of teaching. She was somewhat elated, too. The week was a success. She wrote in her journal on Friday night, "I really believe I am learning to like teaching."

All the same, those early days in the oppressive August heat sometimes seemed miserably long. One particularly hot, rainy Friday night, a couple of weeks later, she wrote, "I took the worst spasm of homesickness and loneliness and discouragement . . ." But the next day she was off on a "jamboree," a picnic, with her landlady's family. Suddenly Bideford, the neighbourhood and her job all looked rosy again.

Bideford lay on the western shore of Malpeque Bay (the other side of the bay from Malpeque where Aunt Emily and Uncle John lived). The school was, " . . . about as artistic as a barn, and bleakly situated on a very bare-looking hill," and inside was "big and bare and dirty." Still, Bideford was a bustling community where there was still some shipbuilding going on, and Maud liked it. Its houses were mostly the white clapboard she was used to. Huge oak and elm and maple trees grew along the red dirt roads. The boats and nets of the oystermen (Malpeque Bay was famous for its oysters) covered the beach as fishing boats did at home and, with the smell and the sound of the sea to gladden her senses, Maud felt she could not be homesick too often.

She boarded at the Methodist parsonage. It was a handsome, white, gabled house and she had a big second-floor room with a window looking out towards the sea. She did not like Reverend Estey all that much—he was a dour man with a sarcastic way about him that reminded her of Grandfather Macneill—but she became great friends with Mrs. Estey and their daughter, seven-year-old Maud. (Mrs. Estey was the absent-minded cook who baked the cake with "anodyne liniment in it by mistake" and gave Maud the idea for the cake Anne Shirley baked when Mrs. Allen came to tea and the sawdust pudding Sara Stanley made in *The Story Girl*.)

Maud worried at first, as she always did in a strange place, that she would be friendless and lonely, but, of course, that wasn't the case. She became "chums" at once with a girl named Edith England. Edith was bright and cheerful. She was engaged to marry a young law student and so had time to "go about" with Maud in the afternoons and evenings and the two young women—and sometimes Edith's fiancé, when he was home—had many a cosy visit and many a companionable walk along the shore of an evening.

Maud fell into a way of life that, except for the teaching, was much like her life at home or her visits in Park Corner. She attended at least one, usually two, church services on a Sunday. She went to dances, skating parties and sleigh rides. She joined the local sewing circle and she went dutifully to church socials. "Church socials," she wrote crossly, after coming home from one, "for downright stupidity . . . take the cake." She made a list of ways one must behave at them in order to get along:

1. Sit prim.
2. Look demure or disapproving according to your age.
3. Hang back and act cranky in any game other people try to get up.
4. Cram yourself with a lot of indigestible stuff, the effects of which will be ever present with you for a week.

She finished by adding, "If I thought I would have the moral strength to keep it I'd make a vow never to go to a church social again!" She liked dances and skating parties a lot better.

Only a few weeks after she'd settled herself at the parsonage, Will Montgomery (one of the Montgomery distant cousins), came to drive her to his home in Port Hill, a few kilometres inland from Bideford, to spend a weekend with his mother and sisters. After that he drove over often to call on her and Maud was always pleased to see him. He was amiable, he was "cousinly" and never "sentimental"and she liked his "intelligent conversation."

A young man named Lewis Dystant began driving her home from choir practice. He asked if he might escort her to prayer meeting. Soon it was church socials and then skating parties and dances. He was good-looking, serious and kind, but Maud considered him not as interesting as Will or as much fun as Edith and her fiancé. But she thought that he did "very well for somebody to drive about with" and she accepted his offers.

It didn't seem any time at all before September became October and there was fall with its "chill, high coloured skies, mournfully-sighing winds, coldly purple seas, [and] shorn harvest fields . . ." Slowly Maud began to realize that she was actually a teacher—and what a hard job teaching was. The day she gave the "fourth class" a written exam in grammar, she wrote in her journal, "I suppose they thought they had a hard time but it wasn't as hard for them as for me!" Remembering the days when she had been a schoolgirl, she couldn't help wondering, " . . . if the teachers I used to think such marvels of learning and dignity really felt as I do."

The teaching may have been hard but it continued to go well. At least it was going better for Maud than her writing was. In the early mornings, in the afternoons after school, and most evenings she wrote in her big room with its window overlooking the bay. She sent her work out to newspapers and magazines but, with only two exceptions—one poem, and one story for which she was paid nothing—the mails brought her manuscripts back to her with those "icy little rejection slips" pinned to them. Twenty-three years later, long after she was an international success, she wrote in *The Alpine Path* that "tears of disappointment would come in spite of myself, as I crept away to hide the poor, crumpled manuscript in the depths of my trunk. But after a while . . . I only set my teeth and said, 'I will succeed.'"

She decided she would have to have more education, so she applied to the Ladies College in Halifax, Nova Scotia. She got a letter from the college principal suggesting that, if she weren't able to take the full course at Dalhousie, the degree-granting college, she should take a "selected course" there. With her Prince of Wales courses, she was too advanced for the Ladies College.

She determined to follow that advice and began to save every penny she could from her one-hundred-and thirty-dollar a year salary. Having that goal in mind helped keep her spirits up but, as always, Maud's moods could shift from high and happy when things went well to black as eternal night when they didn't. In one journal entry, she described the "overcast" sky, the "wrinkled gray clouds, the cold gray shadows settling down over the withered fields," then said, "It made me feel hopeless, and as if the best of my life lay in the past." In quite another mood, she described a sleigh ride with Lou Dystant as, "a dazzle of frost and moonlight . . . The night was bewitching, the roads were like gleaming stretches of satin ribbon, there was a white frost that softened the distant hills and woods to a fairy dream, and the moonshine fell white and silvery all over. I never enjoyed a drive more."

She went to Charlottetown for a few days in winter and saw her friends Mary and Norman Campbell, her cousin Jack Sutherland and some of her old teachers. She went home for a visit and went to a party where she "nearly danced [her] feet off." She went to Park Corner, but felt low because both Stella and Clara were away from home. Frede was still only a child and George just wasn't the companionable, gossipy company the girls were.

What made the visit even more depressing was that Lem McLeod was home in Park Corner and, in spite of all her efforts to keep him from it, he proposed to her one night in the Campbell's parlour. In one way it wasn't as terrible as John Mustard's proposal, because Maud really liked Lem. But, in another way, it was worse, and for the same reason. She really didn't want to hurt his feelings. When she couldn't stop him from proposing, she told him firmly that she would not marry him but that she liked him and hoped he would still be her friend. How she wished that! How she wished that the boys she liked would be her friends and would not get so "sentimental" about her.

In December Uncle John Montgomery had a stroke. Will Montgomery came from Port Hill to take Maud across the bay to Malpeque in January to see him. She was very glad of Will's company and glad not to have to go home alone afterwards, because it was so heartbreaking to see Uncle John in that state. "Could that haggard wasted creature be the big, hearty uncle of yore, with the ringing voice and the laugh that shook the house?" she wrote that night.

He died in February and she mourned him. She had visited in Malpeque often over the years and Uncle John and Aunt Emily were often in Park Corner when she was there. She had loved Uncle John Montgomery from when she'd been six years old and he had come to Cavendish to court Aunt Emily. She had more than loved him, she had been devoted to him from the moment he'd swung her up into his arms and hugged her after she had pounded him ferociously at his wedding for taking her aunt away from her.

The winter seemed never to end but, at last, it was spring. Trilliums and violets bloomed in the woods. Buds came out on the trees. The roads, those "gleaming stretches of satin ribbon," became stretches of treacherous red mud. And the school inspector came to judge the year's work. He asked questions and listened to the children recite multiplication tables and read aloud. He was so well pleased that he gave the school the afternoon off. Maud felt that, indeed, she had learned to be a teacher.

By the end of the school year, Maud had most of the money she needed to go to Dalhousie. She lacked only eighty-five dollars and she wrote to Grandmother Macneill to ask her for it. Grandmother agreed to give it to her. Maud resigned her teaching post and said goodbye to another group of good friends.

Saying goodbye to Lou Dystant proved very distressing. He said goodbye in the front hall of the parsonage after a late meeting. He told her he was in love with her and wanted to marry her. He said that he couldn't help asking her even though he was sure it was hopeless. Maud wrote in her journal that night that she was sorry—and a little cross—because she had made a great effort to discourage him from thinking she cared for her in any way but as a friend. All the same, she may have felt a little guilty because she knew that he felt things deeply and she had let him drive her around all year because it made life easier for her. Lou said goodbye with tears in his eyes.

On the last day of school in June the pupils brought flowers and ferns to decorate the room and brought Maud "a very pretty little jewel box of celluloid mounted in silver" and presented it to her with a speech. Then everyone cried. She wrote in her journal that night, "This has been a very happy year for me and I shall never think of that old school without a very kindly feeling."

CHAPTER 10

Dalhousie

"'Oh,' sighed Anne. 'I can't describe how I felt when I was standing there, waiting my turn to be registered—as insignificant as the teeniest drop in a most enormous bucket . . . I knew I would go down to my grave unwept, unhonoured and unsung.'"—ANNE OF THE ISLAND

Maud went to Halifax in the middle of September with Grandmother Macneill's eighty-five dollars and her blessing—Grandfather would not even talk about where she was going. "Cavendish people generally show a somewhat contemptuous disapproval," wrote Maud in her journal, "Mrs. Albert Macneill, who never cares what she says or how she says it . . . remarked to me the other day, 'I don't see what in the world you need with any more education. Do you want to be a preacher?'"

Maud didn't really care about Mrs. Albert Macneill's opinion, but she wrote in her journal that she liked "Mrs. A. in spite of her shortcomings" and couldn't help feeling "hurt and bruised by this attitude of old friends and acquaintances . . . If I had just one *friend* whose opinion I valued—to say to me 'you are right. You have it in you to achieve something if you get the proper intellectual training. Go ahead!' what a comfort it could be!"

How that mean-minded attitude echoed through all Maud's books in the attitudes of "friends and acquaintances" towards the desires and ambitions of her heroines. So she gave Diana Barry to Anne Shirley and Ilse Burnley to Emily Starr, to be the kinds of friends she had wanted so badly. And, more than likely, when she sent Anne Shirley off to Redmond College in Kingsport and Mrs. Harmon Andrews said sourly, "I don't see that Anne needs any more education," Maud was remembering Mrs. Albert Macneill.

With or without a Cavendish blessing, Maud was on her way to Dalhousie College in Halifax. Her journal entry the day she arrived in Halifax reads, "HALIFAX SEPT. 17, 1895. The date is surely worthy of capital letters!"

The whole year was worthy of capital letters, although it wasn't without its difficulties. Maud hadn't been at the college a week before she wrote in her journal, "I *am* homesick, that can't be denied . . ." but, since she was always homesick the minute she left home, she stiffened her spine and prepared to dive into her year at college.

Although her courses were at Dalhousie, she was to stay at the Halifax Ladies College and, the week before she had left home, she'd received a letter from a girl named Perle Taylor asking to be her roommate. She agreed, but the arrangement did not prove successful for either of them. She wrote about Perle, after they had stopped rooming together, that she still liked her but that they had nothing in common and that she supposed that she'd bored Perle as much as Perle had bored her. It was probably true.

Maud didn't have much respect for the intellect of a number of the girls at the Ladies College. The plain truth was that she really was brighter and quicker and had more imagination than most of them. While she could settle comfortably into a "gabfest" about "dress, beaux and eatables," she wanted—she needed—more than that. She needed companions with whom she could talk about the books she was reading and the ideas that were constantly forming in her mind. She needed a kindred spirit who felt that same mystical connection she felt for woods and streams and sea and sand. Companions who liked to talk about these things were not easy to find and she soon earned a reputation among some of the Ladies College girls for being standoffish and of thinking overmuch of herself.

Maud was as popular at Dalhousie as she'd always been, but this wasn't the first time in her life she'd been labelled standoffish—or even snobbish—by some. She never really understood it. For as long as she could remember (and before), she had been made to feel like a person of no importance. So she could not comprehend, not in that deep part of herself where self-knowledge is found, how her sharp words or even "those looks" she gave, could possibly have the power to wound others. She felt herself to be misunderstood and, in the books she wrote, she did her best to vindicate herself. Many of her heroines—Anne Shirley, Emily Starr, Jane Stuart, Valancy Stirling—are all called standoffish and often accused of being too fond of themselves. And all the book characters who think that of them are thoroughly dislikeable.

But Maud wasn't considered standoffish by everyone either at the Ladies College or at Dalhousie and, before long, she was having a hard time juggling her studies and her busy social life. She paid calls on all her distant Halifax relatives and the relatives of all her Cavendish neighbours.

She was invited to concerts, lectures and parties by other Dalhousie students.

She had her cousin Murray Macneill to thank for one invitation. Murray (Uncle Leander's son) was in his final year at Dalhousie and the girl who was giving the party had a crush on him. She thought inviting Maud would help her chances with him. Maud liked going to parties, so she went, but the invitation made her laugh. Murray, who had spent every summer of his young life in Cavendish at Maud's house, hadn't even bothered to telephone her in Halifax. (She wrote in her journal that it was because he couldn't forgive her "for not bowing down and worshipping him—something which he demands from all feminine creatures.")

Maud made particular friends with two young women: Bertha Clark, who was the housekeeper at the Ladies College, and Lottie Shatford, who was staying in Halifax with her married sister and who, like Maud, was taking only a few of the Dalhousie courses. Bertha was a friend and ally at the college (and had access to the kitchen). Lottie was small and bubbly and seems to have been a bit like Anne Shirley's friend Phil Gordon in *Anne of the Island,* "very loveable" and "not half as silly as she sounds." Lottie and Maud often went walking together in the public gardens along "the gray paths littered with whirls of crinkled leaves" and Maud sometimes went home with Lottie for an evening visit or out to a concert or a Gilbert and Sullivan opera.

She liked Halifax, the old "warden of the north." She loved the romance of a town that had streets and churches and provincial buildings dating back to the eighteenth century. She loved the Citadel on its hill looking down over the town. She liked the

"Greenmarket," the shops on Barrington street, the public gardens and the horse chestnut trees on the walk to the college from her residence. She loved the big, handsome, clapboard houses, so like the ones in Charlottetown. Halifax was older, bigger and offered more interesting lectures and concerts but it was not so very different from Charlottetown—and it was by the sea. She couldn't smell the sea or hear its roar way up at the school nor could she hear it anywhere in the city over the sounds of carriage wheels and horses hooves on the paved streets, but she knew it was there.

Gradually she became accustomed to the college, her professors and the other students. She liked her English courses and she took to shorthand at once, realizing how useful it was going to be to her as a writer. She liked all the courses but Latin; the professor pronounced the words differently than "dear old Dr. A." at Prince of Wales College and she couldn't get used to it.

The days grew shorter, the winds off the sea grew colder, "the moon of falling leaves [was] slipping away" and, early one November morning, Maud woke up feeling decidedly ill. At first she thought it was the crackers and gooseberry jam she'd eaten the evening before with Bertha Clark in the college kitchen. It wasn't. She had the measles. She had to spend a month in quarantine in the Ladies College "hospital . . . a bare, barn-like set of apartments in a remote part of the college . . . and oh, how terribly dull and wearisome it was!" To make the misery more miserable she was quarantined with a girl named Rita Perry with whom she shared a hearty dislike. The whole experience was so awful that the two girls made an unspoken pact to get along and make the best of it. They talked about anything that came to mind and groaned together over the "abominable invalid's diet—weak tea, toast, and various slushes" they were given for the first two weeks.

They were not allowed to get up or to use their eyes during the first week because of the damage measles can cause eyes. When at last they were allowed up and given books and papers, Maud wrote a silly verse she titled *When Perry and Mont had the Measles,* the two of them invented jokes, and they waited impatiently every day for their friends to come to the bathroom window across the courtyard and communicate with the sign language they'd invented. They all—on both sides of the courtyard—jumped up and down, waved their hands wildly, doubled over with laughter trying to make each other understand. At the end of another week the invalids were allowed out for walks but strictly forbidden to go near any of their friends. Then, finally, after being thoroughly disinfected "from head to heels," they were let out, "reeking of cinnamon but happy beyond words."

The first term was nearly over and the school principal, Miss Ker, had had a chance to get to know the girls. She came to Maud and asked her if she'd like to have a room upstairs where the Dalhousie girls roomed. Maud was overjoyed both to be with the "Dal" girls on "pandemonium flat" and to have her own room. She was back in class by the end of November, working furiously to catch up on the essays she hadn't written while she was sick and cramming for Christmas exams—Latin, French, History and two levels of English.

She did not go home for Christmas. Her grandmother wrote that it would be best not to because of the bad roads. Maud wrote, matter-of-factly, in her journal, "I know what that means. Grandfather doesn't want to be bothered meeting me or taking me back." She said nothing more about it. She put her loneliness from her firmly and spent a quiet holiday at school—the only student left there—reading, writing and going for long, brisk walks. Christmas day, she wrote, turned out to be "a rather pleasant one, after all," with gifts and "delightful letters" from friends, "a goose repast and a pleasant evening in the parlour afterwards."

It was spring that brought the excitement that put Halifax in capital letters. The first thing that happened was that she won a contest in *The Halifax Evening Mail*. The newspaper had run a contest in January asking for answers to the question "Which has the more patience under the ordinary trials of life—man or woman?" She had sent them a poem. It began,

"As my letter must be brief
I'll at once state my belief
And this it is, that, since the world began
Since Adam first did say
'Twas Eve led me astray
A woman hath more patience than a man."

and went on for four more humorous verses. The entries were to be sent under a pseudonym so she signed it Belinda Bluegrass. The prize was five dollars.

The letter (with cheque) telling Maud she'd won the prize came on February fifteenth. The very next Thursday she got another cheque for five dollars from a magazine in Philadelphia called *Golden Days,* for a story she had sent them called *Our Charivari.* That Saturday she got a letter from the editor of *The*

Halifax Herald asking her to contribute an article for a special Dalhousie edition of the paper. One week later a magazine called *The Youth's Companion* sent her a cheque for twelve dollars for her poem *Fisher Lassies*. Then, on April second, she got a cheque for three dollars from *Golden Days* for another poem, *The Apple Picking Time*. That night she wrote in her journal, "A restless mood is on me and I cannot settle down to my books." No wonder!

She finished her year with studying and exams, parties, concerts, overnight visits with Lottie Shatford, but no weeks that came after them could match those wonderful weeks in early spring. She felt like a real writer. She wrote in *The Alpine Path*, "Never in my life, before or since, have I been so rich."

In spite of the temptation to go out and buy herself pretty clothes or a wonderfully frivolous knick-knack with her earnings, Maud saved every penny but the five dollars from the *Evening Mail* prize. She wanted something to keep forever from that money so she bought good editions of the works of her favourite poets: Tennyson, Longfellow, Whittier and Lord Byron.

She left Halifax on a "misty grey morning" at the end of April, already missing her Halifax friends at school but immensely encouraged and ready to look for another school in the fall.

CHAPTER 11

I Am Not Maud Montgomery At All

"Anne's plans could not be settled until Roy had spoken. He would soon—there was no doubt of that. And there was no doubt that Anne would say 'yes' when he said 'will you please?' . . . It was not just what she had imagined love to be. But, was anything in life, Anne asked herself wearily, like one's imagination of it?"
—ANNE OF THE ISLAND

Once home from Halifax, Maud put her possessions away in her "own dear den" and made the rounds of all her favourite people and places. Then, feeling those "forty different ways at once" that she always felt when she first got home, she sat down one evening to read the old letters her Cavendish friends had sent her five years before during her year in Prince Albert.

Maud saved all her letters. Often, throughout her life, she would pull her old ones from their keeping place and read them. The sweet sadness of nostalgia was a feeling she never tired of. Her journals are liberally sprinkled with sentences like the one she wrote that night after reading those Cavendish letters: "How vividly they brought back those dear old schooldays . . . a strong longing swept over me to go to those dear old merry days when life was seen through a rosy mist of hope and illusion . . ."

She didn't spend a lot of time indulging in nostalgia that spring. She mailed her applications for a teaching job (her grandfather remained obstinate and would not drive her or allow her to drive). Then, every moment she could spare from chores, she spent with her head bent over the kitchen table or her desk upstairs, her pen scratching over the pages of foolscap that had replaced the old letter bills. The magazine *Golden Days* bought another short story for five dollars and Maud wrote in her journal that some of her friends were beginning to be envious of her good fortune. "I smile cynically," she wrote, "they do not realize how many disappointments come to one success. They . . . think all must be smooth travelling."

Then, on a visit to Park Corner in August, she saw her cousin Edwin Simpson and he had good news for her. He was giving up his teaching job in his home village of Belmont to go to college in October and he'd gotten her the job replacing him. Thankfully Maud went home to prepare for another winter's teaching.

Belmont wasn't nearly as agreeable as Bideford. It was on the southern shore of Malpeque Bay and Maud thought it was quite pretty in October, with the leaves turning red and gold on all the trees along the streets, the sea shining just beyond. But the school was small, it stood on what Maud called, "the bleakest hill that could be picked out" and the children were "terribly backward . . . a scrubby lot of urchins" and she was sure she was not going to like them.

Ed had found her room and board with the Fraser family. Their house was close to the school and it had the post office in its front room. The meals weren't all that good, but the

Frasers were plain, decent people and Maud liked them. Her tiny, closet-sized room off the parlour was "detestable," though. All it had in it were a narrow bed, a washstand, a curtained-off corner for her clothes and a small table with a mirror over it that was so poor Maud wrote that she saw herself in it as she hoped "devoutly that others do not." She put her trunk at the foot of the bed and tacked her calendars and her pocket watch on the walls. She set the china dog that Well Nelson had given her and a photograph of Jack Sutherland on the mantel in the hope of making her cubbyhole cosy.

She might have done, too, if the cubbyhole hadn't been so cold all winter. She often had to sleep in all her clothes with her coat piled on top of the blankets. Once she stole out into the front hall and took a fur coat from the coat rack to throw on top of everything else and, one morning when she woke up, there was snow on her pillow. She hadn't slept in such a cold room since the boardinghouse in Charlottetown during her teacher's-college year.

Maud hated the cold. She wrote in her journal in November, "Cold seems to shrivel me right up. I can endure nearly everything else but if I get cold I am no good for anything physically or mentally."

Worse than the shrivelling cold was that there weren't any convivial young people in Belmont as there had been in Bideford—no girl friend like Edith England, not even a Lou Dystant to drive her about. What was every bit as bad for this lonely girl, for whom letters from friends were a lifeline, was that there were only two mails a week. In Belmont Maud waited in the post office on mail days with the same impatience with which she had once gone to meet the trains in Prince Albert.

Then there were her Simpson relatives. Of all the families in the vast Prince Edward Island Macneill clan, who, as Great-Aunt Mary Lawson said, considered themselves "a little better than the common run," the Simpsons were the worst. They considered themselves even better than the rest of the clan. As well, they all talked all the time and had a habit of "asking you a question and giving you the impression that they are not paying the slightest attention to what you are answering." The Belmont Simpsons, Samuel and Eliza and their seven children, were distant cousins. There were four children still at home: Fulton, Alf, Burton and Sophy. Then, one November day, Ed made his presence felt. Maud got a letter asking her to correspond with him. She thought it was "quite a clever letter," and, because she was lonely, she decided to "agree to an occasional correspondence as it will . . . lend a little spice to this dead-and-alive sort of existence."

The dead-and-alive sort of existence in a bleak, boring village, teaching in a poor school with poorer students and a room to live in that was "as cold as an ice-box" did not improve, despite letters from Ed Simpson and from her friends in Cavendish, Halifax, Charlottetown and Prince Albert. To ease her loneliness, Maud went out to her Simpson cousins whenever she was invited. Great-aunt Mary Lawson was living with them for the winter and Maud loved this great aunt. She loved her for her kindness and because the two of them were true "kindred spirits"—they both had the same sense of humour and they were both story tellers. From the days of her young childhood, Maud had been drawn to Great-aunt Mary Lawson and it was from this dear, wise old woman she learned all the old family stories she put into *The Story Girl, The Golden Road* and *The Chronicles of Avonlea*.

Lamentably, she couldn't spend all her time with Great-aunt Mary Lawson so, dutifully, she sat in the parlour and chatted with the whole family and drove to church with them on Sundays. Very soon those drives—to church, to a social evening or back to Frasers at the end of the weekend—were the means of making the whole family miserable. Not for the first time Maud wished she weren't quite so attractive to boys. Fulton and Alfred began competing to be the one to drive her. She didn't like Fulton, a big, awkward young man (and very "Simpsony") but he became infatuated with her and every time it was Alf's turn or Maud paid Alf any kind of attention, Fulton went wild. He either shouted and stormed around the house saying dreadful things to Alf or closed himself into his room and sulked. He took to staring at Maud long and soulfully. Then he began to spy at her from behind window curtains to see who she was with when she was arriving at or leaving the house. Finally his infatuation made him so ill he took to his bed. He was a long time getting over it. There's no record of how the family felt about Maud as a result of Fulton's behaviour but Maud found it so distressing that she stopped spending so many weekends at his house.

Wrapped in shawls and mufflers, sitting at the wobbly little table in her room, Maud kept on writing but she wasn't selling anything. The children in school didn't seem to be learning anything from her: like Mr. Carpenter in *Emily's Quest* she was "tired of teaching nonentities . . . tired of trying to make soup in a sieve." And she was having a never-ending series of colds and sore throats. She was beginning to be really depressed. She wrote in her journal that she couldn't remember ever having felt so low. Then, at the beginning of February, she got the surprise of her life. Ed Simpson proposed to her.

On the fifth page of a long, tedious letter about his studies, he told her he loved her and wanted to marry her. She was stunned. She wrote in her journal, "I don't seem to be able to believe that this has really happened. Other men have loved me and I have always guessed it long before they told me but it never entered my mind that Edwin Simpson cared anything for me." She read the letter over half a dozen times and still couldn't believe it. True, five years earlier in Park Corner, Ed and Lem McLeod had all but fought with their fists for the privilege of walking her home from Literary Society meetings. But that had seemed like a game. Later, in Charlottetown, Lem had made it clear that it wasn't a game for him, but Ed had never done that. In fact he'd never showed even the smallest hint of lover-like feelings towards her, not even that past summer when he'd told her about the Belmont school.

She couldn't marry him, of course. Or could she? She was twenty-three years old. She was getting nothing but rejection slips for her writing and she was beginning to hate teaching. Her future looked bleak. What's more, married women were socially acceptable. Spinsters were scorned, made the butt of stupid jokes. She told herself that Ed was "very much improved" from the way he'd seemed five years ago. He was tall and handsome, dark haired with dark, penetrating eyes, he was clever and he was getting an education. He was going to be a Baptist minister. The Simpsons *were* one of the Island's leading families, so he would certainly be a "suitable" husband. Her grandparents would disapprove, because Grandfather hated all Simpsons and Baptists and was set against cousins marrying. She wouldn't let that stand in her way, though, not if she loved Ed. But she didn't.

Because it was so cold and dreary in Belmont, because she was so lonely and depressed, and because he was so very suitable, when she wrote him, Maud didn't turn him down flat. She told him she did not love him but that, if he were willing to wait and hope that she would one day feel differently, he might do so. He wrote back that he wouldn't take her answer as a final no. He would wait and hope.

A few weeks later Maud had a letter from Laura Pritchard in Prince Albert to say that her brother Will had died of influenza. Sitting on her narrow bed in the same cold, little room where she had sat and read Ed Simpson's letter, Maud stared down at Laura's lying in her lap. It couldn't be true. Not Will Pritchard, so bright and funny and dear. Remembered scenes flashed in and out of her mind: long walks with Will along the river eating vanilla creams and talking over life's mysteries, Will passing her notes in code, telling her jokes in class, saying goodbye in the spring and exchanging photographs and rings and ten year letters. "We might be reading them together in ten years," he'd said. Now that could never be. She picked up Laura's letter and read it again. Then, with it clutched in her hands, she fell back on the bed and cried until her pillow was soaked with tears.

As she always did in times of stress, no matter what the cause, Maud turned to her writing. It never failed to give her courage. It failed this time. She sold two stories in March but the dreariness of the winter had soaked too deeply into her spirit. In spite of the coming of spring, with the ice breaking up in the Bay and the pussy-willows in bud along the brooks, so like the ones in the Haunted Wood back home, she felt no joy.

Ed's marriage proposal began to seem more appealing. She wasn't persuading herself that she was in love with him. In fact, despite all her flirtations and the one or two "violent fancies" she'd had, Maud had come to really believe that she wasn't a girl who could fall in love. She had her ideal man. He was Anne Shirley's Royal Gardiner "tall and handsome and distinguished-looking—dark, melancholy, inscrutable eyes—melting, musical, sympathetic voice . . ." and, perhaps—with his "ironic tongue . . . lean, clever face . . . with its magnetic green eyes"—like Dean Priest, the cousin Emily Starr did not marry in *Emily's Quest,* and not too unlike Zanoni the storybook hero of her earlier fantasies.

She wasn't even sure she wanted to fall in love. Her writing was too important to her. There might not be time or energy in her life for a husband. But to be married meant not being lonely. It meant not having to teach in schools as hateful as the Belmont school. And there was something else. Ed said he loved her. His saying that had made her suddenly realize how much she wanted to be loved. "So maybe," she thought, "that will make it all right." She didn't write to tell him, but she decided that, when Ed came home from college, if she felt she could care for him at all, she would accept his proposal.

He came home in June. Three evenings later, he walked Maud home from prayer meeting. The moon was bright, there was a soft wind from the sea stirring the pale green leaves on all the trees and the scent of lilacs filled the air. He told her all about his college courses. A perfect night for a proposal of marriage. But Ed talked about the books he was reading, he talked about the weather, he asked Maud about the Belmont school and the church. Then, as they were turning into the lane leading to Maud's boardinghouse, he stopped. He turned to face her.

"I suppose you were surprised to receive that letter of mine last winter," he said abruptly.

Maud's heart sank, she felt a little dizzy. She knew what was coming. She stared up at him. The moonlight shone full on his expectant face. The silence was terrible. She stumbled through a few mangled words and then, so rattled she hardly knew what she was saying, she stammered," I-I think I do care for you. I will be your wife."

"Thank you," he said solemnly and kissed her. Then he asked if he might have the flowers she had pinned to her dress. While he talked happily about his plans for the future, she unpinned the flowers and handed them to him in a complete daze. She knew, already, that she had made a horrible mistake.

She wrote in her journal that that night "marked the boundary between two lives for me . . . the girl before that time was as dead as if the sod were heaped over her . . . I am not Maud Montgomery at all. I feel as if I must have sprung suddenly into existence and she were an altogether different person who lived long ago and had nothing at all in common with this new me. I have been an utter, complete, wretched little fool. I see it all now plainly, when it is too late."

It did seem to be too late. Maud was proud. She could no more have accepted a man's proposal one day only to tell him that she had changed her mind the next than she could run naked down the road in Belmont. For weeks she couldn't sleep, she couldn't eat, she was numb from the knowledge of what she had done.

Everything she felt about Ed's proposal is how Anne Shirley felt in *Anne of the Island* when Roy Gardiner asked her to marry him. "She opened her lips to say her fateful yes . . . she found herself trembling as if she were reeling back from a precipice . . . She pulled her hands from Roy's. 'Oh, I can't marry you-I can't-I can't,' she cried wildly.'" Maybe, as a way of undoing her own disastrous mistake, Maud allowed Anne to realize hers before she made it.

She could not bring herself to behave towards Ed in a lover-like fashion. While he walked her blissfully to and from church and prayer meeting, spoke to her with loving words and fondly kissed her goodnight, she was cold and almost formal towards him. She wrote in her journal that he was like all the rest of the men in his family, so busy talking or thinking about himself that he hardly noticed anything about anyone else. She came to dread the very sight of him.

At last school was over and Maud went home, but she could not escape her folly. Ed came to see her in Cavendish not long after she got home and, after he'd left, she ran up to her room, threw herself on the floor and muttered into the carpet, "I can never marry him—Never, Never!" But she couldn't tell him so.

She wrote poems. She had one accepted by *Munsey's* magazine. She wrote stories. She wrote and she wrote with an almost frenzied need. She read new books and a few old favourites. She had a new grey cat she called Coco: "a plump silver-gray creature." In Maud's eyes, "the only real cat [was] a gray cat." She walked, she spent time with her friends. She wrote letters. She went to Charlottetown to the Agricultural Exhibition and saw Aunt Mary McIntyre and Aunt Maggie Sutherland. She saw Jack and her old Charlottetown roommate, Mary Campbell, but not even that rush of nostalgia could lift the gloom that had settled over her.

Then, in October, she went to Lower Bedeque, a village on the south shore of the Island, to substitute teach for a friend of Ed's named Alpheus Leard while Alpheus was away at college. She boarded with the Leard family: Alpheus's mother and father, two brothers and three sisters. Eighteen-year-old Calvin was not home often. Herman, who was twenty-seven, lived at home and farmed with his father. Two of the girls were still very young. Helen was Maud's age and good company for her. Maud liked them all, and she liked the "lively" town and the little school set in a grove of spruce trees like the one at home.

She began her teaching in Lower Bedeque more contented than she had been since the night she had accepted Ed Simpson's proposal. She had made up her mind she would tell him she could not marry him. But she kept putting off writing the letter because it was so painful. And then she fell in love with Herman Leard.

Herman was slight and dark-haired, with "magnetic" blue eyes. He was "jolly and full of fun" and he and Maud were soon teasing each other and making jokes that had the rest of the family laughing uproariously. Maud liked him as much as any boy she had ever known. Then one night, in the buggy driving home from prayer meeting through the frosty air, Herman put his arm around her. He kissed her and she discovered a "rapture such as I had never in all my life experienced or imagined."

It frightened her. Maud was like Emily Starr who did not want "to belong to" Dean Priest. Like both Anne and Emily, the two of her book heroines most like her, she had struggled valiantly, all her life, against her disapproving relatives to become her own independent person. The overpowering love she felt for Herman Leard threatened to destroy that independence.

There were other reasons why she did not want a romantic attachment to Herman. One was that, even though she did not mean to marry him, Maud was still engaged to Edwin Simpson. She was ashamed. A Montgomery could not "be going with" one man while she was engaged to another. The other was that she did not mean to marry Herman, either. He was a farmer, sweet and gentle and loving, but with "no trace of intellect, culture, or education."

It was snobbery, the kind of snobbery that pride in family and social position brings about, but it was also common sense. By the age of twenty-four, Maud, who missed little that went on in the world, had seen many marriages. She knew that love could easily wither when there was nothing of the mind or spirit to sustain it. "I would be deliriously happy for a year or so," she wrote in her journal," and wretched, discontented and unhappy all the rest of my life." Also, Herman did not like her to write and she knew she could never live without her writing.

So she promised herself, over and over, that she wouldn't let Herman put his arm around her or kiss her any more. But she did let him. She couldn't seem to help herself and she felt as though her heart and soul were being wrenched apart.

Then, in March, in the midst of her torment, Grandfather Macneill died in Cavendish. He had a sudden heart attack on a Saturday afternoon. It was a great shock. But Maud did not pretend to herself, even when he had just died, that she felt differently about him than she always had. "I cannot say that I have ever had a very deep affection for Grandfather Macneill," she wrote in her journal. "I have always been afraid of him . . . Nevertheless, one cannot live all one's life with people and not have a certain love for them . . ."

She went home for the funeral, her thoughts so full of memories of her grandfather and worry for her living grandmother that all other thoughts and feelings were shoved aside. But they returned "to gnaw and sting and burn" as soon as she was back in Lower Bedeque. She knew that there was something she could do to ease some of her anguish and she did it. She wrote to Ed Simpson asking him to release her from her promise to marry him. He answered in a "heartbreaking" letter, twenty pages long, that he could not simply "set her free," that "his love was eternal" and he could not believe that she had ceased to care for him. After writing two more letters, pleading with him to reconsider, brought her the same response, Maud wrote a letter which she, herself, called " harsh and unjust" and was "bitterly sorry" afterwards for having sent it. He wrote, then, that he saw that he had no choice but to set her free, and he sent her back her photograph.

Her passion for Herman Leard couldn't be ended as easily. It was ironic. A few months before, she hadn't slept, hadn't been able to eat because she was engaged to a man she did not love, now she couldn't sleep, couldn't eat because of a man she could not stop loving. She wrote despairingly in her journal, "I have a very uncomfortable blend in my makeup—the passionate Montgomery blood and the Puritan Macneill conscience.

Neither is strong enough to wholly control the other." In the end, the Macneill conscience won out. When Herman's brother Alpheus came back in the spring to take over teaching in the Lower Bedeque school, Maud went home.

On the evening before she left, she sat on the sofa with Herman in the Leard's parlour. A cheerful fire burned in the stove but neither of them felt at all cheerful.

"You'll be taking the school again after Al is done of it, won't you?" Herman asked, his eyes asking so much more than his words.

"I don't suppose I'll be able to teach anymore. I'll probably have to stay home with Grandma after this," said Maud. She couldn't look at him. She couldn't say to him that she would never see him again but, somehow, he understood. They kissed goodnight one last time at the parlour door.

"I thought my heart would break," she wrote in her journal when she was home in Cavendish. "It was all over . . ."

No matter how she tried, she could not shut Herman Leard out of her thoughts or feelings. She was "frantic with longing for a glimpse of his face." She couldn't write. She went on long solitary walks. She breathed her grief into Coco's soft grey fur. She prayed. She wrote in her journal, "I will conquer. I will live it down even if my heart is forever crushed in the struggle."

A year later Herman Leard died of influenza. When Maud described Anne Shirley kneeling at her window at Green Gables in agony over Gilbert Blythe's desperate illness in *Anne of the Island,* she did it knowing, deep in her heart, how Anne would feel. She, too, knelt at the window in her room all night. The "fragrant soft summer air" washed over her but it could not ease her pain. Nothing could. All she wanted, in those dark hours, was to be with Herman forever in his "unending dreamless sleep."

The next day she sat down at her desk and began to write.

CHAPTER 12

The Alpine Path

"She had hours of rapture and insight that shed a glory backward and forward. Hours when she felt the creative faculty burning like a never-dying flame. Rare, sublime moments, when she felt as a god, perfectly happy and undesirous."—EMILY'S QUEST

1900. Maud was twenty-five years old when the new century came in. The light in her grey eyes was not quite as sparkling as it had once been, her tongue was possibly a bit sharper than of old, but she was the same slim, spirited, talented Maud Montgomery. She was asked to recite at "Literary," play the organ at choir practice, invited to "drive about" with one or another of Cavendish's young men, and always had partners to dance with at parties. She was learning to operate her new Brownie camera and friends were after her all the time to take "snaps" of them. She made a darkroom out of the spare room upstairs so that she could do her own developing.

Many of her old friends had moved away. Over the years she had grown a little apart from Amanda and Lucy, and Pensie had married. She had no real "chum" in Cavendish now. It didn't seem very important. What she wanted more than anything were her trees and garden, rambles alone through "the lazy, dappling shadows" of Lover's Lane and down by the rocks and sand to watch the "silver-tipped waves" roll in—and to sit with her cat by the window in her room where "the winds drift by with clover scent in their breath . . ." She was still getting used to her home without Grandfather in it, still feeling the echoes of the stress and her feelings of remorse about her engagement to Ed Simpson. It was only a year since Herman Leard's death. But she was writing.

She was writing steadily. In one of her journal entries, she declared in a tone of deep pleasure, "How I love my work. I seem to grow more and more wrapped up in it as the days pass . . . Nearly everything I think or do or say is subordinated to a desire to improve my work." She was selling both poems and stories regularly to magazines and journals in Canada and the United States. Cavendish neighbours, like Aunt Ruth in *Emily Climbs,* "gave up, finally and forever, all slurs over wasted time." In fact, many of them had become envious. And now they were afraid she would put them in her stories. Sometimes she did, too, although not always in an obvious way. In her story *The Softening of Miss Cynthia,* about the ill treatment of an orphan boy, some of her local readers must have cringed a little. In *Miss Sally's Company,* about snobbish girls who can't be bothered with a lonely old aunt, Maud may have had a few of her own cousins in mind. But she didn't always set out to portray her neighbours. With Emily Starr in *Emily's Quest* and her indignant letter from "Second-cousin-once-removed Beulah" who "thought she might have spared an old friend" Maud must often have thought, "If I had thought of Cousin Beulah, I most certainly wouldn't have put *her* in a story."

She was too busy to spend much time thinking about what her neighbours thought of her. Grandmother Macneill was now in her late seventies and so crippled with rheumatism she could do almost nothing. Maud didn't mind taking over the duties of postmistress. She didn't really mind the sweeping and dusting or keeping the oil lamps filled and their wicks trimmed, either. She liked to cook and she loved the garden. She didn't mind lugging the wood for the stoves in from the wood pile, or keeping the fires going or cleaning out the ashes. What she did mind was the time it all took. And Grandmother was becoming very hard to live with. She would go into a rage if Maud wanted to stay up past nine o'clock, and was jealous of the attention Maud paid guests. She may have been in the early stages of senility or Alzheimer's Disease (a disease undiagnosed and not understood at that time) but all Maud knew was that she was very difficult.

Then, early one bitter cold morning in January, there was a telegram from her step-mother in Prince Albert. "Hugh J. Montgomery died to-day. Pneumonia. Peacefully happy and painless death."

Clutching her dressing gown with one hand, Maud stood at the kitchen door, heedless of the wind whistling through the cracks, looking stupidly at the telegram in her other hand. Automatically she crossed the room, poured water from the steaming kettle into the teapot on the back of the stove, threw in a handful of tea and sat down at the table. It couldn't be true, she thought, it just couldn't be true. There had been a letter from her father only days before full of cheer and proud words about his "Maudie" and her literary successes.

She couldn't even cry, her grief was so terrible. This was worse than Herman's death. Even though Father had lived far away, they had always been "near and dear in spirit." Now he was gone. She had nobody "except poor old Grandmother." For weeks she was in such despair she couldn't even write.

But, after a time, Maud being Maud, her chin went up and her old determination thrust itself forward and she took stock of herself. "Well, I must henceforth face the world alone," she wrote in her journal, "Let me see what my equipment for such a struggle is. I am young . . . I have three hundred dollars—Father left me two hundred in his will and I saved another hundred these last two years. I have no training for anything save teaching, which I cannot at present do; I have no influence of any kind in any quarter. Is that all? . . . Yes, there is something else—my knack of scribbling. Is it a feather's weight—or is it a talent of gold? Last year I made exactly ninety-six dollars and eighty-eight cents by my pen! That does not promise extravagantly. But we shall see. I have forgotten to mention another asset and a very valuable one—a belief in my power to succeed. As long as I possess that I shall face the future with an unquailing heart."

With a small portion of the three hundred dollars, she bought herself a second-hand typewriter and taught herself "to manipulate it." Day after day, with the sunlight filtering through the lace curtains in the sitting room, night after night, by the glow of the oil lamp, she pounded away at her new contraption at the big, oval table with Coco sleeping on her feet where he always slept while she wrote. She poured her heart into poetry but, when a good plot came to mind, she enjoyed writing stories. They were potboilers to earn money—love stories, ghost stories, stories of sad little orphan children. Although she no longer wrote romances about high-born lords and ladies in distant lands (like Anne Shirley's *Averil's Atonement),* many of them were about people with social position and wealth. Not all of them. Maud was gaining confidence in herself and her skill. She was beginning to write about what she knew and understood, stories set on farms and in villages on the Island, about people you could know. They had heroines with Maud's own backbone, Maud's love of nature (and of cats), her own tastes. Some of them were early versions of books that came later.

In a story called *Jane Lavinia,* about a young woman who gives up a career as an artist in New York to stay home with her lonely aunt, there is a scene where Jane Lavinia, obeying her aunt's orders, "took off the chiffon hat and pinned on the sailor with bitterness of heart." This story not only reflected its author's love for the chiffon hat. Enlarged, changed and suited to Anne Shirley's character, became the basis for *Anne of Avonlea* and it shows up again in *Emily Climbs,* when Emily does not go to New York with Janet Royal. When Maud got her hands on a good story idea, she didn't let it just wither and die, she got every last bit of good out of it. In *Aunt Susannah's Birthday Celebration,* two of the characters called Anne and Gilbert have a dreadful quarrel and are so stubborn they almost do not get married. The quarrel between Anne Shirley and Gilbert Blythe that goes on through three of the *Anne* books probably began in this story.

A story called *Freda's Adopted Grave* is about a child who cannot put flowers on a grave on "Graveyard Day" because she is an orphan from far away and has no grave to put flowers on. Stories about lonely, rejected children, like this one, foreshadowed the Anne and Emily stories, *Jane of Lantern Hill*, and many of the stories in *The Story Girl, The Golden Road* and *Further Chronicles of Avonlea*. It was, after all, a story Maud knew all too well.

Maud was not exaggerating by much when she lamented that there was no one left for her except Grandmother. Her Campbell and Crosby aunts, uncles and cousins in Park Corner and the relatives in Charlottetown who cared about her were too far away. By now, they all had telephones, but long distance charges were too great for daily or even weekly calls. She had Coco (Grandmother had not only given in to having cats indoors, she had come to dote on them) but Coco could not relieve the gloom that had overtaken her.

Her Macneill relatives were no friendlier, no kinder than they had ever been. Maud wrote in her journal that Uncle John Macneill (whose farm was next door) was a "domineering, insulting, unjust, bad-tempered man, without one spark of consideration for the rights and feelings of other people." Aunt Ann Maria was as cold and uncaring as her husband. She had always treated Maud with disdain and she seemed to enjoy making up malicious stories about her. Lucy, who had been so close a friend in childhood, now did the same. (Maud knew this because a gossipy neighbour had related them to her during a sewing circle one afternoon.) The boys, Prescott and Frank, who once upon a time had tagged along on fishing trips with Maud and Dave and Well Nelson and to whom Maud had written many letters from Prince Albert, had grown up to behave as their father did.

When Uncle Leander and his family came in the summer for their six-week vacation, or Uncle Chester and Aunt Hattie came from Charlottetown, Uncle John and Aunt Ann Maria "never showed their meanness." Like Emily Starr's Murray clan in the Emily books, Valancy Stirling's clan in *The Blue Castle,* and the terrible Pringles Anne Shirley had to deal with in *Anne of Windy Poplars,* the Macneills put up a good front for visiting family and for outsiders. Maud must have often wanted to be an outsider because, when she was with those relatives, she, who was such an accomplished talker, whose wit was as swift as lightning, whose own tongue could be as sharp as a needle, was "ill at ease and tongue-tied."

Early in 1901, *The Charlottetown Daily Patriot* had in it an article about Island poets and there was her name "written out in cold-blooded fulness—'Lucy Maud Montgomery,' the foremost of the younger school of writers.'" Maud was greatly "chuffed" by the recognition of her growing success but it wasn't what she needed at that time. She needed to get away.

In August she was offered her chance, a winter-long job as proofreader for *The Halifax Morning Chronicle and Daily Echo.* The pay was five dollars a week. Prescott agreed to stay with Grandmother for the winter—"too ashamed to refuse," was what Maud thought. Grandmother agreed she could take the job and she accepted it, not at all sure she was doing the right thing.

She left in November. In spite of her usual homesickness for the Island, it was good to be back in Halifax. Almost the moment she stepped off the train, she was walking in the public gardens and peering eagerly in the shop windows along Barrington street. She had joyful reunions with her friend

Bertha Clark, who was now working as housekeeper at the Halifax hotel. She went with Lottie Shatford on long walks and poked around their old classrooms at Dalhousie. She established herself in a comfortable boardinghouse and was soon settled into a routine.

She went to church on Sundays. From Monday through Saturday she was at the paper, reading proofs for mistakes in spelling or grammar until 2:30 in the afternoon with an hour for lunch. After that she answered the telephone, did odd jobs, made friends with the cats who prowled around on the roof outside her office window, and went out on assignments the reporters didn't want or hadn't time for. On an afternoon when she had less to do than usual, she was prowling among the newspaper's books and papers and came across *A Bad Boy's Diry,* all about "Little Gorgie's" mischievous doings. She loved it again as she'd loved it at the age of nine but, this time, she howled with laughter over it.

One day she was assigned an article about a hat establishment and its owner was so delighted with what she wrote that she insisted on giving Maud a hat, "and a very pretty one, too." She wrote a weekly column for *The Echo* she called *Around the Tea Table,* about everything from fashion to food fads, and signed it "Cynthia." Once she was asked to "trim mercilessly" the last few draggy installments of a novel being serialized. Not long after it was printed, a fellow staff member remarked during a casual chat that the story was very strange. It had wandered on and on for weeks and then, just like that, finished off as smartly as a marching band. Maud did not enlighten her coworker about its authorship but she recounted the incident in her journal and it appeared, almost exactly as it had happened, in *Emily Climbs* when Emily works for the *Charlottetown Times* and does that same thing to the story *A Bleeding Heart* and Mrs. Rodney says exactly what Maud's co-worker said. (Unlike Emily, Maud never received a visit from its enraged author.)

At first Maud tried doing her own writing in her boarding-house room at night, but she was too tired. She got up at six in the morning, but it was too cold and she was too hungry. "Now, Maud, what are you going to do?" she asked herself— and came to the conclusion that she would have to fit her story writing in and around the proofreading, the phone answering and the hundred-and-one noisy things going on in the news-paper office. She managed to write—and sell—quite a few stories that way.

When she left the paper at the end of May, she was prom-ised that she could have the job again the next winter. It felt good to get the offer, but she knew that she wouldn't be going back to Halifax, even though she also knew she would never "have another chance" like it. Grandmother was miserable with Prescott. He had been nasty to her all winter, letting her know, in every possible way, that he did not want to be with her. "He was always a cad," wrote Maud angrily in her journal, "and a cad he will be to the end." She went home.

Grandmother was glad to see her. Coco, the cat, was glad to see her. She was glad to see Grandmother, glad to see Coco, glad to send Prescott packing, glad to be home again and sleeping, once more, in her "own dear den." And that fall she made a new "bosom friend": Nora Lefurgey, the teacher at the Cavendish school.

Nora could talk about religion, politics, poetry, novels—all the things Maud so loved to talk about—and was fun besides.

They walked around Cavendish taking pictures and they laughed and giggled like little children together. And, together, they wrote a mock diary—Maud would write in it one day, Nora the next. It was full of jokes, "humorous sketches" of things that happened in Cavendish, and cartoons they drew themselves. Their friendship lasted all their lives, even though they hardly ever saw each other after the next June when Nora gave up the Cavendish school. Maud hated to see her leave but, in one way, it was a relief. Grandmother's jealousy of any of Maud's friends was making it impossible for Maud to invite anyone home and difficult to spend time with them elsewhere.

Grandmother's behaviour was growing odder and more intractable. Now she wouldn't have any heat in the house except in the kitchen until both she and Maud nearly froze all winter. "A state of freezation," Maud called it and she resented it terribly. She was often so edgy she was close to tears but she dared not show it for fear of one of Grandmother's rages. As the months wore on, how she wished herself back in Halifax, but she couldn't leave her grandmother. Maud, at thirty, had the same strong sense of what she owed her family as she'd had five years earlier when she had said goodbye for-ever to Herman Leard. Also, as difficult as Grandmother had become and, as cool and distant as she had always been, she had never been mean or stingy. Quite the reverse, she had always seen to it that Maud had everything she needed. With the help of Maud's father, she'd bought her the organ to play on and, more important, she had helped Maud get to Prince of Wales College and to Dalhousie. She was the only mother Maud had ever known and Maud loved her.

Spring lifted Maud's spirits. The apple trees bloomed right

outside her bedroom window, filling the room with the scent of their blossoms. They drew her out into the garden, where the daffodils seemed to have captured the sun in their golden clumps and the smell of the fresh earth was intoxicating. And beyond was the woods, where the little waxy, pink trailing arbutus grew under the snow that lingered in the shadows of rocks and dark trees. It was impossible to be glum surrounded by all that magic.

Before her winter in Halifax, Maud had begun exchanging letters with a woman named Miriam Zieber in Philadelphia, who was starting a literary circle by correspondence. Miss Zeiber had given Maud's address to two aspiring writers, an Alberta rancher named Ephraim Weber and George MacMillan, a Scottish journalist. They both wrote to Maud and she answered both. Corresponding with these fellow writers was like finding a shady brook in a desert. Here, suddenly, where there had been nobody, were the kindred spirits who understood what she was doing and why. Here were the people who knew how hard it was to get words down on paper and uncompromising black ink in a manner that was even a distant echo of the beautiful ideas in one's mind. Here were people who understood the pain of a rejection slip, the surge of joy when a story or a poem was accepted for publication, the feeling of triumph at seeing it in print.

Maybe these fellow writers spurred her imagination. Maybe it was the coming of spring that did it. Something did and that something started a book going in Maud's head—although, at first, she didn't know it was going to be a book.

She was sitting at her desk in her room one night looking over the notebook in which she kept her story ideas. She came across a note she'd jotted down ten years earlier, "Elderly couple apply to orphan asylum for a boy. By mistake a girl is sent them." The couple were Maud's Cavendish cousins, Pierce and Rachel Macneill. Ellen, the baby they'd been sent, was now fifteen years old and sometimes came to sit with Grandmother when Maud had to go out to a meeting or to church. Maud had never been close to Ellen but, in that moment, reading that note, she felt that "flash" of excitement that usually came with a new poem. This time it was a story.

Feverishly she began to block out the story, invent incidents for it, "brood up" its heroine. The heroine she was "brooding up" was nothing like Ellen Macneill. In fact, Maud decided she wasn't going to be exactly like anyone she knew. She would have red hair and a quick temper and her name was going to be Anne Shirley. From that point Anne began to take over and Maud grew so fond of her that she thought it was a shame to waste her on a short story or even a full-length magazine serial that would wouldn't last beyond its final episode.

"Write a book about her," Maud said to herself, "You have the central idea and the character. All you have to do is to spread it out over enough chapters to amount to a book."

She thought about her book. She dreamed about it. She wrote whole chapters of it in her head. She knew this was not a story just to keep the pot boiling and it was not going to be a stiff moral tale, either. Her Anne was going to be "a real human girl." Maud always insisted that Anne had not been modelled after anyone, she was original, real. "If I turned my head quickly should I not see her," Maud wrote, "with her eager, starry eyes and her long braids of red hair and her little pointed chin? . . . I have always known she was somewhere."

Of course Maud had always known she was somewhere. She did not have red hair or quite the flashing temper Anne had, but right down to those starry grey eyes and that pointed chin, Anne Shirley was Maud Montgomery with all the passion and stubborn determination that went with those features. Anne's story was not Maud's, but the loneliness that brought about Katie Maurice, Anne's window friend, was Maud's loneliness, and Katie Maurice was Maud's window friend, even to the name. Anne's hatred of her red hair was Maud's longing for curls. Her love of pretty clothes and of unusual and difficult words was Maud's love of those things.

In May she began to write the book—on her typewriter that "never makes the capitals plain and won't print 'w' at all." She wrote it all summer, she wrote it all fall and winter and, as with Emily writing *The Seller of Dreams,* "Nothing mattered but her story. The characters came to life under her hand and swarmed through her consciousness, vivid, alluring, compelling. Wit, tears, and laughter trickled from her pen. She lived and breathed in another world . . ."

The following January, it was finished. Into it went the heart and soul of Maud's own life, her passion for trees, for the wind, for the sea. There, unchanged, were her Lover's Lane, her Haunted Wood, her Lake of Shining Waters. There, renamed Avonlea, was Cavendish itself. Green Gables was copied—with changes—from David Macneill's farm, across the road and up the hill from where Maud lived. She insisted that neither David nor his wife Margaret were models for Matthew and Marilla Cuthbert. She had made Matthew a shy old man so that Anne's effervescence would stand out in contrast, but David Macneill was an extremely shy man and, maybe, without realizing it, Maud *was* influenced by him when she created Matthew.

Pierce and Rachel Macneill's house became Mrs. Rachel Lynde's house. Rachel lent Mrs. Lynde her first name—and probably Mrs. Albert Macneill, who prided herself on always speaking her mind, lent her her personality. Diana Barry was likely a combination of Amanda Macneill and Laura Pritchard. Josie Pye, Jane Andrews, Tillie Boulter and Ruby Gillis were combinations of all the girls Maud had grown up with in the Cavendish school, as Gilbert Blythe, Charlie Sloan, Moody Spurgeon MacPherson, Glover and Ned Wright were of the Cavendish boys—although Gilbert may have owed something to Will Pritchard as well. The Avonlea teacher, Mr. Phillips, who was "dead gone" on Prissy Andrews, was very like John Mustard, the Prince Albert teacher who had proposed to Maud. As for Miss Stacey, Anne's "true and helpful friend," Maud said herself that she was inspired by Hattie Gordon, her own beloved teacher.

The Avonlea friendships, the hostilities, the rivalry for top place in school were those old Cavendish days of Polly and Molly, of Snip and Snap, of Maud and Nate. There they all were, the colours, shapes and sizes of those old friends and companions, mixed and tossed up in Maud's imagination, to emerge on paper as the living characters of the fictional Avonlea.

It was January 1906, when Maud wrote "'God's in his heaven, all's right with the world,' whispered Anne" and pulled the last page from the typewriter. *Anne of Green Gables* was finished.

CHAPTER 13

Anne—And After

"But it was the little parcel that was responsible for her excitement . . . Emily knew what it must hold. Her book . . ."—EMILY'S QUEST

Anne of Green Gables was not published the year it was finished. With loving care, Maud, like Emily with *The Moral of the Rose* in *Emily's Quest,* "typewrote it faithfully and sent it out. It came back. She sent it out again, three times. It came back." Only, unlike Emily, this time Maud did not retype "the dog-eared thing." She had a good cry and stuffed it away in her clothes closet in an old hat box. One day, she knew she would trim it as mercilessly as she had trimmed the serial in the *Halifax Morning Chronicle and Daily Echo* and send it to a Sunday school paper. But not right away.

Something else was going on in Maud's life in 1906. Through all the time she had been living as much in Avonlea as in Cavendish, her "outward" life had taken on a new and surprising turn. She was being courted again.

Ewan Macdonald came to Cavendish late in the summer of 1903 to be the minister of the Presbyterian Church. Maud was writing and she was struggling to keep herself from falling into a depression which even summer and a new dark grey kitten named Daffy could not keep at bay (Coco had disappeared, "the fate of so many roving Thomases"). She wasn't spending much time thinking about the new minister, although she did say in her journal that he was young, probably not much older than she was, and "fine looking with thick black hair and black, roguish eyes, a pleasant smile" and the Gaelic accent common to the descendants of the Scottish settlers at the eastern end of the Island.

She saw Mr. Macdonald in church and at choir practice that year but never at social gatherings because he was boarding in the next town and didn't get to Cavendish in the evenings. His absence from their social affairs did not stop the local gossips from speculating about him. A handsome man like that! A bachelor minister! One of the Cavendish spinsters was bound to snag him.

One thing Maud knew. It was not going to be her. She had no desire to be a minister's wife. Furthermore, she liked Mr. Macdonald but she thought he was a bit shy and awkward and, whenever they happened to chat together, he didn't seem interested in anything that interested her. She decided she wouldn't encourage even a friendship with him. Then, two years later, he moved to Cavendish to board at Laird's, the farm behind Uncle John's. Over the next year Maud saw him often at social gatherings and, because he lived so near her, he began driving her to and from the more distant ones. And, of course, he came to the post office. Maud would give him his mail and then he would stop to visit, sometimes for over an hour. She discovered, as the minister got over his shyness, that they had more in common than she had thought. She liked him better and better.

During those hours she spent with him in the post office, they talked about books they were reading, about theology, philosophy, the Island's history—never about love or marriage. Nor did he speak to her or look at her like a man in love. All the same, Maud had a feeling that marriage was on his mind. If she was right and he proposed, how would she answer? She was not the same girl who had so disastrously accepted Edwin Simpson's proposal nine years earlier. She was almost thirty-two years old now and had known the sadness of love lost. She knew she was not in love with Ewan Macdonald but she had grown truly fond of him. She wrote in her journal that she felt "the loneliness of . . . life more keenly when he went away." A home of her own with companionship would be so pleasant. And she wanted children. A "workaday, bread-and-butter happiness," might content her very well. But what if it didn't? What if, after she'd married him, she fell in love with someone as she had been in love with Herman Leard? What if Ewan did?

Then, one day in the spring of 1906, Ewan told her he was resigning from the church. He was going to Glasgow, Scotland to take more courses in theology. He would not have the Cavendish church when he came back to Canada. Just like that, the decision was made for Maud. She did not want him to disappear. He had come to belong in her life. She would marry him if he asked.

He did ask. He proposed to her one rainy October night while he was driving her home from a social evening at a neighbour's. With the rain beating on the leather buggy roof and dripping down in front of them from its edge, he said to her, "There is one thing that would make me perfectly happy . . . It is that you should share my life—be my wife."

"I will marry you if you are willing to wait until I am free," Maud told him, "I promised my grandmother I would never leave her and, as long as she lives, I must stay with her."

"I will wait," he said.

Ewan went to Scotland. Maud kept house and wrote. And all the time her life had been taking this interesting new turn, Anne Shirley had been sleeping in her hat box. One winter afternoon, a few months after Ewan left, Maud came across her story while she was rummaging around in the attic clothes closet for something. She began "turning over the sheets, reading a page here and there." She liked it. She liked it every bit as much as when she'd just finished writing it. "Why shouldn't other people like it, Daffy?" She pulled the cat out of the closet where he was busy rummaging where she'd left off. "Why not try once more? Why not?" And, once more, she wrapped *Anne of Green Gables* in paper and string and sent it out, this time to the L.C. Page Company in Boston.

In the middle of April a letter came from the Page Company saying that they wanted *Anne of Green Gables*. Not only did they want it, they wanted a sequel as soon as possible.

Maud was standing in the middle of the kitchen. The sun was streaming through the window. She looked out at the bare trees and thought she had never seen anything so beautiful. They wanted her book! And a sequel! She, Lucy Maud Montgomery of Cavendish, Prince Edward Island, Canada, was going to have her name on the cover of a book. She pinched the letter, she squeezed it, she pressed it to her heart. Then, terrified she was going to tear it, she smoothed the lovely, heavy cream-coloured paper with her hand, folded it and held it gently by one corner. "Oh, how proud Father would be," she thought.

With a deep, happy sigh, Maud grabbed her shawl and shoved open the door. Hiking her skirt up to her knees, still clutching her letter, she raced like a child down the road to Lover's Lane. There she confided in the catkins on the pussy-willow trees and knelt down and whispered to the brook, "My dream has come true. The dream I dreamed so long ago at my old brown school desk, it's come true! I have a book!"

On the last day of June, *Anne of Green Gables* arrived in the mail, a handsome book with a painting of a grown-up, rather elegant Anne on the cover, a book to hold, to turn the pages of, to slide between two other books on the shelf. "Not a great book at all," wrote Maud, being scrupulously honest with herself, "but mine, mine, mine."

Maybe not a great book, but it was such a success that, almost immediately, while Maud was hard at work on its sequel, it went into a second printing and then a third. By the end of the year it had gone into six printings. It was reviewed in newspapers and journals in Canada, the U.S. and Great Britian and was very soon being translated into almost every language in the world. The first royalty cheque was for seventeen hundred and thirty dollars, an enormous amount of money for a young woman who had, only seven years earlier, worked for the *Halifax Morning Chronicle and Daily Echo* for five dollars a week.

Over the next few years, letters poured into the the post office in Grandmother's front room. Devoted readers wrote that they were reading *Anne of Green Gables* over and over again, they loved it so. Fan clubs were started everywhere and girl babies from Poland to Australia were being named Anne or Shirley. Mark Twain wrote her that Anne was "the dearest and most loveable child in fiction since Alice." Maud was thrilled.

Even the Macneill relatives were impressed, if not by the book itself, certainly by Maud's fame. Some of them, like some of her neighbours, were so full of envy they muttered about "poor, old spinsters who had to do something with their lives," and "girls who always thought they were better than everyone else."

"Just write a successful book or do something they can't do," Maud wrote to one of her pen pals, "I could not begin to tell you all the petty flings of malice and spite of which I have been the target . . ."

In September 1910, Earl Grey, the governor general of Canada, wrote and asked to meet her during a visit he was planning to Charlottetown. What an occasion that was! It was a triumph even before it took place. Word of the invitation shot through Cavendish like a bullet. The Sunday before Maud went to meet His Excellency, friends gushed over her in church and the envious gossips had nothing to say.

Great-aunt Mary Lawson was staying with one of the Cavendish relatives. She insisted on going home with Maud to look at the invitation and admire the celebrity in her flower-trimmed straw hat and the beautiful brown silk dress she'd had made for the great day. "Such an honour," sighed Great-aunt Mary, happily, "such an honour for the Macneill family!"

The next day Maud took the train from Hunter River to Charlottetown. There she met the earl, his countess, their daughter and their aides. From there, the party took a special train to Orwell, where a writer named Andrew Macphail lived. They had an elaborate afternoon tea in the glassed-in verandah of the Macphail house, then the governor general asked Maud to go for a walk with him so that he could hear all about her books. Maud liked the earl. She described him in her journal as "a tall, genial, elderly man with a frank pleasant face and a most unaffected 'homely' manner." She told him how *Anne* had come to be, about the sequel, *Anne of Avonlea,* about *Kilmeny of the Orchard,* which had just been published, and about *The Story Girl,* which she was still writing.

He listened attentively while they strolled through the apple orchard and along a winding path beyond. When they came upon "a neat little building painted white with a lace curtain in the window," he lowered himself to the step and invited Maud to sit beside him. She was horrified but she simply could not bring herself to tell him that the pretty little building was the Macphail outhouse. She wrote later that she could only suppose the earl had never heard of outhouses.

They sat there talking for over half an hour. Maud was trying so hard not to laugh that she was not her usual animated self and the earl finally asked her if she had been nervous about meeting him.

"Yes," said Maud, "I've been in a blue funk."

The earl laughed. "Well, you won't be anymore, will you?"

"No," Maud answered, steadfastly not looking at the "straggling twos and threes of women stealing through the orchard in search of the W.C. and slinking hurriedly back when they beheld the Earl." As they got up to leave, even while she was gravely promising to send His Excellency a copy of *Kilmeny of the Orchard* and all her poems, she was controlling a giggle with great difficulty, wondering if "some poor soul" had been stuck inside the outhouse all that time. The rest of the visit was everything proper that a visit with the governor general of Canada and his family should have been, but none of it was even half as interesting as the talk on the outhouse steps.

Excitement followed excitement. In November of that same year, Maud went to Boston for two weeks to see her publisher. By this time, the L.C. Page Company had already published the second *Anne* book, *Anne of Avonlea* as well as *Kilmeny of the Orchard*. Now they hoped to publish *The Story Girl* and they had invited Maud to Boston to meet them personally. After an agony of indecision about leaving Grandmother, Maud decided to go.

She hired a girl to stay with Grandmother and left Cavendish for two weeks—two whole weeks, the longest she had been away from home since her winter in Halifax nine years earlier. It was a trip to "fairyland." She was treated like royalty by the Page family. A notice had been sent to the *Boston Herald* to say that the author of *Anne of Green Gables* was in town and Maud was besieged with invitations to teas, dinners, receptions, concerts and entertainments. She went shopping for beautiful clothes. One "afternoon dress of old rose cloth, hand embroidered in pink silk" cost eighty dollars, more money than she had ever spent on clothes in a year. The extravagance, after all those penny-pinching years, delighted her. It was, in Anne's words, an epoch in her life.

The two weeks flew by. She was home again, feeling a little as though she had been taken out of her cupboard, dusted, polished and put back. So much for fame. She settled down to write about her adventure to Ewan, who was back in Canada at a church in Ontario, to her friends and to her pen pals, Mr.

Weber and Mr. MacMillan—and then to finish *The Story Girl*.

Grandmother died the next spring, in March 1911, at the age of eighty-seven. Early on the morning of the funeral, Maud went into the parlour alone. She looked down at the body of her aged grandmother in her coffin as she had looked down on the body of her young mother from the height of her father's arms thirty-five years earlier. In that moment, she could hardly remember that Grandmother had become so odd and so hard to live with. Maud was grief-stricken. She felt lost. Grandmother had been the one constant person in her life. Softly she whispered, "Goodbye, Grandma." She went out of the parlour and shut the door, "shut it on the old life with all its sweet and bitter," forever.

Before the week was over, she had cleared out the house, packed up her personal belongings, picked up Daffy and left Cavendish. She went to stay with Uncle John and Aunt Annie Campbell in Park Corner, where she would be married. Aunt Annie, Frede, Stella and Clara threw themselves into preparations for the wedding on July 5th. They helped Maud buy the materials and sew the gowns and suits for her trousseau. They made everything for the banquet to be served after the ceremony. Ewan arrived from Ontario. Finally the day came. The three girls helped Maud dress for her wedding. It took place in the parlour. There were twenty-two friends and relatives present to share in the celebration and to wish the newlyweds Godspeed.

The Macdonalds sailed to England and Scotland for a ten-week honeymoon (in an antique shop in England, Maud found a pair of china dogs just like the ones that had been in Grandfather Montgomery's house). When they got back to

Canada, they settled into the manse in Leaskdale, Ontario, where Ewan's church was.

Maud went back often to visit but she never again lived in Prince Edward Island. In a way, though, she never left it, not in a way that really mattered, not in her "inward" life, the life that created six more *Anne* books, another collection of Avonlea stories, a sequel to *The Story Girl*, three *Emily* books, and one more Island novel. Only *The Blue Castle* and part of *Jane of Lantern Hill* are not set on the Island. And all her books, most especially the *Anne* and *Emily* books, are Lucy Maud Montgomery living and reliving, shaping and reshaping the Prince Edward Island childhood that had meant so much to her.

She wrote directly about herself in the book she said was her own favourite, *The Story Girl*. In it, just after Sara Stanley has finished telling one of her magical stories, Cecily says, "I wish there was such a place as fairyland—and a way to get to it."

"I think there is such a place and I think there is a way of getting there, too," the story girl answers.

Their author says, then, "Well, the story girl was right. There is such a place as fairyland—but only children can find the way to it. And they do not know that it is fairyland until they have grown so old that they forget the way. . . . Only a few, who remain children at heart, can ever find that fair lost path again; and blessed are they above mortals. They, and only they, can bring us tidings from that dear country where we once sojourned and from which we must evermore be exiles. The world calls them its singers and artists and story tellers; but they are just people who have never forgotten the way to fairyland."

Maud Montgomery was one of those people who never forgot the way to fairyland. Out of her fairyland, "those dear old days" she loved so much, she brought to life a time and place that have become dear to millions of people all around the world. Surely she has to be called one of the "blessed . . . above mortals."

Afterword

Maud and Ewan Macdonald had three sons. Baby Hugh died the day after he was born, but the other two, Chester and Stuart, grew up in Leaskdale, Ontario, were educated, married and had children of their own. The Macdonalds lived in Leaskdale until 1926, when they moved to Norval, Ontario. In 1935, when Ewan retired, they moved to Toronto where they lived in a house Maud named "Journey's End." Maud died on April 24, 1942 at the age of sixty-seven. She was buried in the Cavendish cemetery near the site of her old home, in a spot she had chosen for herself. In her own words, it "overlooked the spots I always loved, the pond, the shore, the sand dunes, the harbour." A year and a half later her husband was buried beside her.

Green Gables and the land surrounding it, once David and Margaret Macneill's home, is now a national park. On that land there is a monument to Lucy Maud Montgomery, where the devoted readers of her books come from all over the world by the thousands every year to soak up the atmosphere of the island she loved.

Lucy Maud Montgomery's books have been translated into almost every language there is. Three movies have been made of *Anne of Green Gables,* the first a silent movie in Hollywood in 1921, the second a "talkie" in 1934, which was so popular that the Hollywood actress who played Anne legally changed her name to Anne Shirley. The third movie, made in 1985, was a Canadian television serial, with Canadian actress Megan Follows playing Anne, followed by a sequel based on a combination of *Anne of Windy Poplars* and *Anne of the Island*. It was so successful that the film-maker, Kevin Sullivan, created a television series, *The Road to Avonlea,* based on Maud's short stories in *The Story Girl, The Golden Road* and *Chronicles of Avonlea.* He followed this in 2000 with a sequel to the two *Anne* films, a series called *Anne of Green Gables: the Continuing Story,* not a story Maud Montgomery would have recognized (or probably sanctioned), but honouring the continuing popularity of her most famous character.

Kevin Sullivan followed his successful *Anne* films with a production of *Jane of Lantern Hill.* The only other Montgomery books to be filmed have been the three Emily books: *Emily of New Moon, Emily Climbs* and *Emily's Quest.* They were filmed as a Canadian television series in 1998 as *Emily of New Moon.* A televison special, *Lucy Maud Montgomery, the Road to Green Gables,* about her life, was made in 1974 to celebrate the centennial of her birth—and an *Anne* Canadian postage stamp was issued the following year. Countless plays and musical plays have been based on *Anne of Green Gables.* There is an annual *Anne* festival every summer in Charlottetown, and in Japan, where Maud's stories are hugely popular, two theme parks have been opened. At the end of 1999, when lists of the twentieth century's favourite writers were being compiled in Canada, the name Lucy Maud Montgomery led all others.

ACKNOWLEDGEMENTS

While I read many books by and about Lucy Maud Montgomery, Green Gables and Prince Edward Island, I feel I owe a special debt to *The Selected Journals of L.M. Montgomery*, edited by Mary Rubio and Elizabeth Waterston (Oxford University Press).

As well, I am particularly grateful to Jeffrey Kelly for having the patience to listen to me read through the several drafts of this book, and to Grace Clements for the computer that did (as she said it would) make the work easier.